WHEN
"I" Might Be,
WHERE
"We" Are, or
WHAT
You Will

CONCERNING:
MULTIVERSAL PERSONKINDS
AND 'SELF-CONSCIOUS'
SEMANTIC SORT

RUDOLPH MCNAIR

authorHOUSE®

AuthorHouse™
1663 Liberty Drive
Bloomington, IN 47403
www.authorhouse.com
Phone: 1-800-839-8640

Published by AuthorHouse   09/12/2014

ISBN: 978-1-4969-4025-4 (sc)
ISBN: 978-1-4969-4026-1 (e)

FOREWORD

I've bounded bravely off the rocky upland of undergraduate learning, where my studies began, pondering self-consciousness and common sense and fearlessly, then, leapt into speculative space (reaching for ideas about volition and reasoning). In a strange new territory I've dallied, where simple mindfulness might cross good sense, in order to find the proper bearing from which to approach truth.

Unfortunately, I can't commend the importance of what will be writ by me here, but invite the reader to be entertained by the intellectual daring of it, or to be inspired to puzzle with me through the trying inquiries undertaken by better minds than mine to whom I refer. I've discovered no especially surprising truths but, with an oddly slanted reflection and shamelessly blithe commentary, I'll follow a line of reasoning that might not otherwise have been taken.

By the way, I doubt that any supercession of reasoning can be accomplished by defaulting on reason itself or that thinking about some nothingness is possible, and I insist that 'nothing is not knowable'. Such curious speculative impasses as trying to think of "nothing" can confuse one's reasoning (making it doubtful whether negative conceptions might designate some extra-linguistic thing unauthorized by the terms that try to express it) and bear heavily on simple logic. I'm afraid I haven't entirely resisted the temptation to try untangling such knotty snags, but I've usually suffered the grim consequences of doing so. There is, I suppose, no shadowy, transcendental idol lurking behind our history and we must take full responsibility for lifetime's unfolding.

The reader should beware that this study will present a dangerous course to follow, as one must carefully avoid blind alleyways that might confound the unwary (romanticism, for instance, if Hegel is right) and bridges to nowhere (such as solipsism) when asking what self-consciousness and person-being might mean and why we should think so.

I've sought to prepare the ground for a discussion about awakened/enlivened personkindness. "What are individual selves?" I ask, and "are they any different from what I'd 'identify' as some other individual thing?" In order to know what *persons* may be and whether self-consciousness is all that is required to make these personkinds complete. I propose "sociality" (with psycho-social and dialogical components) is a sort of harmonious lyrical composition reverberating throughout life. Conclusions might be drawn from my work that might have political as well as philosophical gravity.

I'll discuss the dialogized heteroglossia (where/how language takes shape) that Mikhail Bakhtin's discussed, and suggest that there are many streams of "meaning" with strong social currents, into which members of any language group might wade. I wonder whether any idea of 'solid' literal ground upon which a particular societal "identity" might stand is entirely cogent.

My meditations are clearly troubled by a frowning distaste for the meager dualism sometimes baked into any metaphysician's delight (cooked up for self-serving reasons, no doubt). I favor more appetizing and/or intellectually spicy feasts. I'll disregard the standard philosophical recipe, therefore, while maintaining that no analytic admixture of 'pure' academic subjects is necessarily satisfying. No delicious cosmography of "covering laws" is prepared for intellectual consumption here, but I hope the wide breadth of my studies prove, nevertheless, palatable.

There have been extraordinary scholars who've often enlightened my way, and I will rouse some of them for help with the task ahead.

(1) Richard Wollheim, <u>The Thread of Life</u>, an especially masterful study of 'living' as persons, from which I shamelessly quote, as well as in-depth investigation of subjectivity, intentionality and the inner world of persons I found fascinating.

(2) Eli Hirsch, <u>The Concept of Identity</u>, who offers a clever explanations of persistence and continuity that proves useful to remember.

(3) Alvin Plantiga and Saul Kripke, <u>Naming, Necessity and Natural Kinds</u>, where one encounters the problem

of 'identity cross possible worlds' (essays: "Transworld Identity & Worldbound Individuals" and "Identity & Necessity") and other important notions.

(4) Baruch Brody, <u>Identity & Essence</u>, providing much to consider about 'knowing', in general.

(5) Danah Zohar, <u>The Quantum Self</u>, whose interesting notion of quantum consciousness is inspiring, if not conclusive.

(6) J. Williams Miller, (a) Midworld of Symbols and Functioning Objects, (b) The Task of Criticism, which clears away much of the philosophic muddle about sorts of 'presence'.

I have no doubt that, beginning at the heel of such formidable authorities, drawing my own conclusions would probably overtax a poor intellect. Nevertheless, by an admittedly 'scissors-and-paste' method, I will try to sort through the relevant evidence that can be got for-oneself (*erfahrung*, perhaps?), discover which applicable facts might be clearly thought of/by-oneself (or *anschauung*?), and recognize the appropriate expressions about-oneself (*Sachverhalt*, so to speak) to which I should pay close attention while taking care not to ignore other serious thoughts (whether oblique or just difficult to translate) that a philosopher-type like me will find fascinating.

IS IT JUST ME ...?

To begin, be advised that I have thoroughly embraced the philosophical method of investigation that presumes the following:

"...The philosopher appears blind and clairvoyant. He lives within this mixture of oxygen and combustible gas which we call the 'True' but he doesn't deign to package truths, not even for distribution in the schools or textbooks. He does nothing but dig deeper, nothing but allow himself to flow, alive, into the ludicrous abyss in order to seek within himself the door opening onto the night of what is not self. This is to define philosophy as meditation, in the Cartesian sense of the word, which means an endlessly sustained tension between existence and being. In order to think one must also be..." (Sartre)

The clumsy speculation I'll begin here may prove too awkward to bear, even for the few pages that follow. Nevertheless, I set out, mustering what serious attention I can spare to give the idea of a *thinking-self* thinking mostly about itself. In due course, I hazard some entirely earnest conjecture about how fully fledged person-being might enjoy the blessing of "sociality", and what good that might be. Unsettling my confidence, still, is that glimpses of *'self'* and *'person'* I'm looking for appear only vaguely in the reversed reflection and dim insight I have about "myself". I can't help but ask whether, by some insidious psychological device, one-self might be locked into a peculiar person-being from which release would otherwise (by dint of whim or sincere displeasure) be wished. I have misgivings about the integrability of person-kind(s) with our like which might trade willing freely away from my lone self (will or no). And, I wonder, too, whether any confident discovery can confirm when rudimentary embryogeny originally demonstrates person-being (if neither clever imagination nor moral sense seem able to say), or why.

I will consult expert academic writ to determine what "individual" selves are and whether selves are in any way different from other "individual" stuff. I suppose that distinctly autonomous person-being will maintain both *willing* and *conscience*, securely identified as "my own" cognition (dialogically). Of course, I suspect these are neither fully sufficient determinants of "one-self" nor merely auxiliary aspects of personkinds (if the maddening subtlety of most truth prevails). If, as some argue, all the perplexing conditions distinctive of individual persons are essential to them then I'm discomfited, somewhat, by how doggedly an unhappy predilection or unmerciful act might work to irrevocably "fix" one's persona (or their 'demeanor').

For convincing reasoning I often refer to John Williams Miller, who outlines the challenge here: "The humanist may ask, 'Well who wants to draw the portrait of a person

as if it were an account or reproduction of an object '?
'No' he says, 'we deal in subjects, minds or persons –
not in things'...of course, if the humanist thinks that
way, he lacks the basis for claiming any general scientific
acceptance. Perhaps he does encounter subjects, minds,
egos, etc., but the scientist is not prohibited from turning
away, saying that he has never encountered a subject. 'Let
those who say they have encountered such things talk
among themselves' but not to him" (6a).

As a cautionary tale; I remember when muddling
through the wearisome sameness of life, while transfixed
by telecast entertainments, I happened once upon a
supposedly madman's fancying about "apexes of thought
in space" (and that fascinated me). You should be advised
that my curiosity is relentless and, that night, I dreamed
of such curious "thoughts" about thinking snapped
free from the confines of the mundane and dazzling
brightly over mindscapes of my naïve imagining. The
idea of disembodied thought relentlessly puzzled me. I've
wondered whether "thoughts" had, or otherwise known,
can escape the familiar appurtenances of brains, and I've
vowed that neither the nature of such strange thoughts
nor the immature brain trying to think them will rest
easily bound in the pitiful confusion from which they
must be released by sheer force of reason!

What is usually helpful when explaining a misunderstood
fact, my professors often reminded me, is discovering
its defining concept or a primordial event (final cause)
out of which the fact arises (Posterior Analytics). I don't
remember any similar forewarning that the definition
of selfsame "souls" would be so confusing, however. I
stubbornly attempt to identify any particularly curious

"thing" by observations which mark out its boundaries. In this way I would be sure to recognize the particular sorts of attributes that operate as one type or order of object. Unfortunately, the descriptive boundaries marking off the edges of personkind(s) of things can be indefinite, at best, and only somewhat clearer over time (how much is sufficient to be one?). I can distinguish its operational whole (encounter it) only intermittently, so to speak, across disturbingly unruly stretches of life-time. Therefore, I wonder if it is one sort of thing at all.

What should I think is either extant or epistemic about such things as "*selves*", and what unreasonable? If, as we are taught by science, our "sensations" require monitors (brains) and the monitoring of that sensibility **is** consciousness then is my "mind" only a matter of integrated brain states, perceptions and reactions? Am "I" in here somewhere running things, or only another predictable part of the whole lot?

The question can also be put as Derek Parfit did, when explaining "Personal Identity" (The Philosophy of Mind, Oxford Univ. Press), thusly: "does personal identity just consist in bodily and psychological continuity, or is it a further fact independent of these continuities?" Parfit thinks there are two answers. He says there is, on one hand, a "complex view that can put one-self together by aligning properly all the instances of it (because, I suppose a complex effort is needed to set selves straight, lineally) And, an alternative, "simple view", he says, holds that *one-self* means just an oddly super-physical and un-analyzable fact. He admits that both ideas are suspect.

The concept of soulful selves that emerged under the auspices of the major religions, I'd add, has been doctrinally complex, perhaps disturbingly so, needing more private introspection than might prove wise. We would now find the ecclesiastical concepts of psychogenetic selves very strange. Not only was one held responsible for impulses and deeds, by their reckoning, but always risked falling victim to supernatural beings hovering invisibly nearby who can overwhelm embodied selves for wicked purposes. Although ours is still a nominally religious civilization there is a telling difference between the historical church cannon describing such oddly imagined spirits and common notions accepted in current thought about ourselves. Of course, many peculiarly 'spiritual' superstitions still prevail, as we shall inevitably discover.

As the son of a Protestant pastor, my religious inclinations struggle to maintain the idea that the body is only a carnal repository (forma corporeitatis) for a supernatural soul for which one has moral responsibility. Nevertheless, I have sometimes blasphemously defended the apparently scientistic idea that soulful "selves" arise, in petto, from the very workings of nature. Moreover, I've entertained the shameful notion that the cosmos is sensitive to the way that it is "lived in", becomes observed, is known or is spoken about. Although a sinful admission, I must admit that I can even dare to imagine that the Catholic Pope, himself, might be mistaken to insist that the sanctity of life obliges any expectant mother to endanger herself, or obliges us to breach her self-possession, unmercifully strain her answerability or to remove her from the safety/privacy of her private (psychological) operative "space" - where and/or when her choices are to be made or become - in order to arbitrarily award that space to a troublingly impersonal sub-letter. I don't doubt that sometime after 'conception' the precious bionomic bud must, at a confidential psychological turn, be granted autonomy within the phrenic fracturing of its caretaker's pregnancy. I suspect that, in this way, a woman's private choices can be daysprings from which the deep stream of personkind-ness flows and upon which private (fudaetal) experiences will float.

Being fully subjective is undoubtedly a more complicated matter, I'm sure, than simply identifying some freeloading "soul" with which one must be stuck.

FOR THE TIME BEING...

The idea of time, generally, is poorly understood even during our finest moments of reflection. Time could be said to be constructed uni-directionally relative to one-self, but casts a "cosmic shroud" of quantum uncertainty over life-world. It can be vaguely re-created but resists being compounded in thought/consciousness.

In a chapter of his book entitled "Living", Richard Wollheim" [1] concedes that a person (one-self) leads life at a crossroads where past and future meet. Wollheim insists that the question about the "timing" of life is at the heart of understanding coherent "self-identity". We are assured this, logically, thusly: if self = f, then when f might occur or it might be the case that sometimes f will not occur, we can discover the facts which contribute to fulfilling f.

I agree that this posture of "hanging between" the flux and flutter of life is especially important to remember. Consider the timeliness with which *person–being* arises. Eugene Gendlin*, for instance, favors Heidegger's conclusion that there are three moments of experience (past, present and future) merged in self-consciousness, and the development of spirit is a *bringing oneself back* from being lost in ongoing reality. He writes; "I can only take over the being I already am by finding myself, and moving forward from this self-finding. We find the person, not at all as some spot or steady entity, but as this finding-oneself. Its essential nature is not to be a 'substantial thing' but, rather, being-in and being-with that is, therefore, fundamentally open to events. What we are is our living; and that is how we are affected differently than a stone is affected. A stone isn't affected essentially. It is a stone, and then it may be changed in this way or that, while its stone-ness continues. Humans are affected. Our being, in Heidegger's view, is always being affected, and that is how we 'find' ourselves…our being rides on the events, is dispersed in what happens, is the being-in what happens" *(Heidegger and Psychology, Review of Existential Psychology & Psychiatry, 1988.).[7]

I'm convinced that I can find *person-being* threaded along life-time; not sewn straightforward throughout but happening to trace a pattern in the tapestry of perceptions, thoughts and actions when/where "I" can be subjunctively woven (involved).

Carnap (der Logische Aufbau der Welt, 1928), in a different way, was determined to show how "life-timed" events can be simplified in "instantaneous total experiences". Having a facetious nature, I'm tempted to ask how much a supposed totally fulfilled instant must include, and for whom? The duration of these 'total' moments must surely be metaphysically primary (immediate/instantaneous) and their psychological resonance basic (memorable). Perplexing, to me, is how on serious inspection such episodes seem to occupy unruly stretches of discernment, memory or imagination and appear with surprisingly different grades of clarity. Sometimes it's thought, as I have, that a more trans-lucid view of "life-timed" occurrences can be invoked here;

"The world in its occasions is here-and-now, the specific and present. It is in contrast to the impersonal, anonymous, inexorable, predictable, uniform, universal – all those polysyllables! It is the light I now see on this paper, and the present memory of an orange in a Christmas stocking. This immediacy is a locus of the private and the personal, and is not to be looked for in wave-lengths, or in the divine omniscience of all times and places. But, neither is it found without light and without oranges and calendars. The 'this-here-now' buys its presence in the established market. It invokes a situation. Occasions require situations and, I would add, situations require occasions..." (6a)

I think that what Miller (above) concludes here is, simply, that any occurrence, however disjunctive, is situated in its reflective perspective and its context (its' *now*). I'm told that any "individual person" can be discovered by finding the manifold of episodes within the context of which some personal perspective will cogently verify familiar features, modes or aspects of things. Moreover, I expect I might find that some such perspectival intuitions are special, nodal apperceptions. Because the general scheme into which a manifold of important/memorable episodes can be organized is the unity-function "lifetime", on this account, from many events taken in proper order and relationship we can deduce (or remember) a lifetime has been "lived" by someone.

WHAT SORTAL FOOL AM I ...

Wollheim tries to convince us that we can "retrace" *person*-being(s) by virtue of sequences of interrelated in-life episodes.

"First we deconstruct a person's life into parts. These parts will be temporal parts and, conversely, anything that decomposes into temporal rather than spatial parts must be a person's life. The temporal parts into which a person's life decomposes are appropriately thought of as events; they are events of the kind that make up a person's life. Then the second thing is to try to find a relation that holds between any two such events, just in case they are parts of the same life. Thus the question, 'what is a person's life?' is answered by looking for a unity-relation for a life. A unity-relation is the relation that holds between any two parts of the same life. And, from the start, it must be conceded that any such relation is likely to be highly complex. In other words, it will state that the different events in a person's life will be connected by this relation, or by that relation, or by the other relation; and, in stating what these relations are, it will place such intransitive relations as 'is' or 'contains a memory of' with the transitive 'is the last member of a sequence of events, each of which is connected with its predecessor in the sequence by being or containing a memory of it'…" [1]

Inter-relational (constructionist) theories, of the sort Wollheim proposes here, are either psychological or corporeal.

An example of an inter-relational psychological theory would be one which holds that two events are events in the 'same life' if, and only if, they belong to a sequence in which any pair of neighboring events can be arranged where/when a latter one not only follows logically from a former but contains a memory of the earlier one.

An example of an inter-relational corporeal theory, alternatively, would be one which holds that two events are events in the same life if, and only if, they belong to a sequence in which any pair of neighboring events are spacio-temporally continuous (empirically conjunctive).

Let's sort all of this out, shall we.

There is, I've discovered, a contingent (adventitious) view of reality which we must sometimes consider. Proponents of this idea try to explain away the supposed coherence of *person*-being altogether. They do not admit that the happenstance of experiential events is logically overcome by any appeal to a notion of simple *identity*. They dare to ask whether the self-sameness of persistent objects is merely fictitious.

"Let me try to broach this idea by way of the following example. Imagine that a tree persists intact during a two day period, from Monday to Tuesday, and that nothing out of the ordinary happens to the tree during that period. Let *S1* be the succession of object-stages corresponding to the tree's career during those two days. The tree will, of course, have a trunk. To be vivid about this, let us imagine that this is a one-branched tree, consisting of nothing but a trunk and one branch. And, let *S2* be the succession which corresponds to the trunk during that two day period. Now comes the somewhat weird part.

I want to consider the succession *S3* which consists of the Monday-portion of *S1* followed by the Tuesday-portion of *S2*. *S3*, in other words, is a succession which consists of the tree-stages of Monday followed by the trunk-stages of Tuesday. Let us consider whether *S3* corresponds to the career of any object as ordinarily conceived. Very evidently it does not; *S3* is, in fact, a mind-boggling path which we can barely get ourselves to think about…an illicit shift occurs in this aberrant path, insofar as such paths combine an object-stage of one sort with an object-stage of another sort. An object may, of course, change in the course of its career, both qualitatively and locationally, and these changes, so long as they are continuous, may even be quite drastic. But, the present suggestion is that it is part of our concept of object-identity that, throughout all of its changes, an object must at least remain an object of the same sort."[2]

Eli Hirsch, as noted above, settled on the idea that matters-of-fact can be arranged in a very commonsense manner, by making what he calls "sortal-covered" judgments. A term is a "sortal" just in case it covers a succession of object-stages (or situations, perhaps) which logically correspond to a persisting object – if it picks out one soft of object rather than another. An object remains an object of the same sort, according to Hirsch, if throughout the course of its career it remains qualitatively and locationally "non-dispersive".

Can we untangle a particular *person*-being from assurgent events into which it is integrally knit if, perhaps, we can carefully sort out just **who** is thread throughout? That seems to beg the question. But, lets' not be hoodwinked about the ordinary identity schemes we want to understand here. I don't think essential *person*-being arrives on the scene when just a suitable set of interrelated events occur (as one might have mischievously intertwined events of dissimilar lives, without breaking the rules of right construction). Of course, we do enjoy a sneaking acquaintance with the truth of things when we pay attention to 'sort' episodes of personkind-ness in ways that minimize confusion.

George Herbert Mead, (The Social Self, J. of Phil, Psych & Sci. Methods, 1913)[8], showed how memory must reintegrate self-sameness into lifetime. He explained that happens when we must 'remember' what in the world was of particular importance to us (personally). Unfortunately, he concludes that "where we are too intensely preoccupied with the objective world the accompanying awareness of self disappears".

For these or other reasons, I suppose, ideas about *persons* "being themselves" comes mostly from academic psychologists (who offer "parallel ratiocination", "memory networks" or "conditioned frames of mind" by which they say *person-being* can be discovered at work) when explaining our thinking processes. Even the most conservative understanding of *person-being* must admit that the knowing-self is more than just sensitivity and instinctive response. Whether concerning "knowing" or "knower" or the "knowable", nothing that has slipped from thought before will escape without our worrying after it, now.

MIND - FULLY FRAUGHT ...

With regard to thinking about thinking (that epistemological adventure), I offer the following: "When Paul and Peter wake up, and recognize that they have been asleep, each one of them mentally reaches back and makes connection with but one of the two streams of thought which were broken by the sleeping hours. So, Peter's present instantly finds out peter's past, and never by mistake knits itself onto that of Paul. Paul's thought, in turn, is as little liable to go astray..." (William James)

A more cosmological slant of mind might also tease the imagination by wondering if any attempt to approach one-self must inevitably descend toward a peculiar metaphysical singularity (by virtue of the "gravity" of any private reality, I'm sure) where most logical rules will break down, to torture the metaphor a bit, and find that it is at the event-horizon of a singular "self" that person-being is orbitally spun.

One may encounter an annoying impasse here. If individual *identity* is only a fact that satisfies some 'natural tendency' to make order from confusion, as some suggest, then why worry about whether it is so? There is the prospect that psychology of this sort minifies the understanding of oneself, by insisting that it is simply an unavoidable adaptation that we think about ourselves as we must do. I find little discursive subtlety shown by psychologists (like Margaret Mahler, who studied how children get a sense of individual *identity*), who propose a simple "drive" toward individuation that is an innate given. On their account, the ordinary way of thinking about oneself is tied to our operational sanity. What Mahler found in this regard was a sense of indentifying introspection that recognizes the rightful place where "I" stand(s) sound of mind.

However important the re-cognition of one-*self*, alone, may be for providing a placeholder in psychological explanations, there are myriad of other mental phenomenon that selves manage to attribute to their *person-being* (such as "rationality", "temperament" and "disposition"). As for mind in the wider sense, one brings "mind" to bear on our problems, or has a "mind" to do this or that, or a mother can "mind" her baby in the same way one must "mind" one's step; so that there surely seems to be something idiomatically substantial, so to speak, and ontogenetically significant about "mind". Moreover, whatever is undergone, *person-being* re-minds one-self what to be, I guess.

I'll hazard a dangerous aside here regarding autonomous *person-being*. I don't believe that personkind-ness is a static fact, nor that person-being begins in any distinct or simple moment. Personkind-ness seems, rather, to eddy and pool in liquid lifespans, where the toe of attention can be dipped (from time to time). I am convinced there is no instantaneous point (like conception) when embryogeny simply "turns on" mental sensibilities.

It should be clear now that any adequate explanation of *person-being*, for my liking, must rely on some account of "mental" activity or other. There are many possible attributes of mental phenomena, but Wollheim considered exactly five worthy of discussion, namely *intentionality*, *subjectivity*, *psychic force*, *quality of consciousness*, and *significance*. [1]

Although I unfailingly miscalculate the 'psychic forces' at play in my own life, with regard to the other attributes he mentions, unless I'm mistaken, the intentionality of a mental phenomenon is its "thought content" (the thought-about). Some investigations conclude that mental phenomenon need not have intentionality and they usually site sensations as examples that do not require thought content. Subjectivity of metal phenomenon means "how" it is made available to the subject or "what it is like" for the subject to experience it (blame Thomas Nagel for that definition). Significance, more importantly (for Wollheim, and for me) is the private meaning that metal state come to have for a particular person. He proposes that some mental phenomena have "iconic" meaning. This kind of mental state has a causal efficacy or force over the doings of persons who have them – building consequently into dispositions to have them, I assume.

"... the influence of the past is carried by mental dispositions that are set up in the person and persist. Examples of such dispositions would be beliefs, desires, emotions, memories, and phantasies. Standardly the influence passes through persistent mental states in which the disposition is manifest. This can come about in two ways. One way is this: the past can color the mental state. The other way in which the influence of the past percolates through mental states requires the past to be more obtrusive. The past doesn't merely color the present mental state, but it or its delegate comes to occupy it, and the person is aware that this is so. This happens in recollection or in memory."[1] Such iconic dispositions are presumably incorporated into a particular personal "character" over time.

Wollheim's notion of iconic mental states is made clear by way of an analogy with theater/spectacle and relies heavily on his vivid literary style. Behind the curtain, we are privy to the philosopher's "stagecraft": "Modeling an account of some part of a mind on an account of the theater will, I hope, allow us to see certain things about the mind that we might otherwise miss. But, this neither has nor pretends to explanatory force. For example, roles are filled by persons, but not necessarily in a one-to-one correspondence. On the same occasion the same role may be filled by more than one person, but on successive occasions more than one role may be filled by the same person" [1]

Finally, we are sitting again in the dark, observing the acts when *person-being* must confess (sotto voce, of course) that it is lost with no rescue in the scene from a menacing drama into which it has strayed. Actual things, remembered things, fearful or lovely things, may all have their veiled and mysterious attributes, yet, since anything is also "my thing", asking what is so-and-so apart from me is to destroy it. Miller calls, this "concrete naturalistic idealism" and insists that it prevails as hard truth.

"This concretism abolishes the controversy over independence which was waged in the interest of prying off the knower from the objects. The physical world is our mental world. My mind is the things or meanings making up my outlook. Any object is defined by its relations and reactions ie., in terms of how it affects and is affected... in relation to human objects this writing is mine, and yours provided any 'you' should peruse it. The mind is not something in my skull but in yours just as much, and in all objects. Mind is not cooped up in the brain case but is abroad in the world or rather it is the world." (6a)

I find myself stumbling around, near the truth here, but can't quite reach the theoretical light switch. I guess the play's the thing.

SPOKEN FOR ...

"To have meaning or to mean something is the basic character of all consciousness which, for this reason, is not just experience in general but a meaningful 'noetic' experience. Consciousness is not a title for psychological complexes, or fused components, or bundles, or streams of sensations which, meaningless in themselves, cannot in any quantity whatever yield meaning." (Ideas of Pure Phenomenology, Edmund Husserl, Allen & Unwin, 1958)[9]

Alternative to the psychological analysis of Wollheim, others think that *person–being* is an engagement in what they call a semantic project (or metaphorical transgression, as Paul Ricoeur calls it) which supposedly dislocates one from what is 'already-in-place' (commonplace?). Therefore, the meaning of "person", he surmises, arises from communication that re-orients one's commonplace experience 'around' someone (lifetime recalled for-oneself).

Ernst Cassirer (The Philosophy of Symbolic Forms III, Yale U, 1985)[10] tries to make what is called a "linguistic turn" in the understanding of person-being, by saying;

"Man not only thinks the world and understands it through the medium of language; his whole intuition of it and the way in which he lives in this intuition are conditioned by this very medium. His grasp of an objective reality – the way in which he sets it before himself as a whole and forms, divides and articulates it in particular – none of this would be possible without the living energy of language."

Heidegger who thought about language as the medium of thinking, insisted that thinking about language "overturns" (his term) itself. He assumed that language is a medium for showing (pointing out) what is not language [ie. Being]. Language/discourse, I agree, is an element in the ontological structure of human-being and, as Heidegger puts it, a "human disclosure" of a worldly manner of being. Heidegger also uses Rede or 'speaking' to add three important ideas about language; namely, 1. what is talked about (idea), 2. the said-as-such (symbol or utterance) and 3. the communication itself (intercourse). He decides that talk about *person-being* itself as an interpretation of a set of signs carrying meaning in discourse.

Other helpful linguistic analysts conclude that proper names are clusters of familiar descriptions that "fix" (affirm) the reference to something, "rigorously" so, eventually, given a proper name. They arrive at these "rigid designators", thusly; "What may be the case is that we fix the reference of a term by the use of some descriptive phrase(s) – but, once we have this reference fixed we then use the name rigidly to designate the referent identified by the descriptive phrase. Once fixed, we do not then take the name to be synonymous with the description

Rudolph McNair

but, instead, we use the name rigidly to refer to the object discussed". [3]

"Naming" alone cannot cover the whole gamut of identifying exercises that might be undertaken (I'm better with faces) but, as Kripke suggests, I'm sure that we have no trouble taking proper names as metaphysically primitive.

Baruch Brody warns that Kripke's designators (names) may not be as 'rigid' as one might think. "… at least some of the objects that we perceive do endure through time and do persist across possible worlds. However, while we perceive their endurance through time, we do not perceive their persistence across possible worlds. I saw my chair yesterday and will see it tomorrow. In this way, we perceive the endurance of enduring objects. However, while I can see that my chair is blue, I cannot see that it might have been red. In this way we cannot perceive the persistence of objects." [4]

Perhaps one can become confused about to whom, exactly, one means to refer when the circumstances where the referent occurs confounds us. For example, a person surely meant could transform into some befuddling counterpart if settled confidence about where that definite one would be found gets replaced. The difficulty here bears, I think, on the distinction between *possible* and *actual* modes of experience, and which happens. Although I cannot pursue a deep understanding of "possibility" here, I'm sure any confusion here is unnecessary. To explain; it seems clear to me that, when using the might idiom, any number of factual conditions can account for whether "f might be/do or might have been/done x". The only difficulty is to be sure which facts are responsible for the relevant actuality to be so.

One must also recognize, I think, which workings of the world might bring about the salient conditions (situation) that operate constantly across time that satisfy an honest apperception of what/who f is, when supposedly certain apperception of operator and operation can adopt the "ontic modality" (Husserl) of presumed, questionable, or doubtful, etc., as one wills. If the chair I might have bought (given my typical desire for another than that in which I'm dissatisfied) might have been painted another color as my likings often imagine but, regardless, such a "possible" object is as functionally (dialogically) lucid for me as one from which I might now arise.

"Rigid" designators, such as my proper name, I've learned are "fixed" (or "situated", if you will) within a constellation of determinations (context) wherein the referent ("Rudolph" for instance) can be discursively deployed. And, I must say that the confidence I have of the truth of this dispels some cynical doubts I've had about my own intuitions, imaginings and discourse from time to time. I'm confident that the semantic mirror in which my image is represented persists across possible worlds and across time, without any dark recesses hidden behind its glamour, or ghostly caretaker holding my place (in reverse).

FUNCTION AT THE
JUNCTION ...

At this point (resistance is futile) I should be convinced that self-sameness is not some loosely related set of stages nor just a kernel of supernatural sentience but, rather, it is a nexus of various lexical references to "one-*self*" with a central psychological theme. I surely have the tools required to decipher the conundrum at hand now, haven't I? But, alas, stubborn scientists like Francis Crick (co-discoverer of the structure of DNA) have finally decoded another clue. They imagine that consciousness (mental activity) could essentially concern a kind of "disturbance" of bionomic equilibrium in the brain, a subatomic "song" played at high frequency energies in each cell of the body, like instruments playing an apparently seamless symphony. Thus our suasion might be re-turned from formal (software) back to final (hardware) causes of coherent consciousness.

"We may ask whether the close analogy between quantum processes and our inner experiences and thought processes is mere coincidence. The remarkable point-by-point analogy between thought processes and quantum processes would suggest that a hypothesis relating these two may well turn out to be fruitful. If such a hypothesis could ever be verified, it would explain in a natural way a great any features of our thinking" (Quantum Theory, David Bohm).

A scientific turn of focus by writers like Danah Zohar reveals an idea about consciousness coming from so-called "new physics which, on this account, might be an interesting interplay (Gestalten?) of material forces. She beings as follows:

"Is consciousness really 'matter', or is 'matter' really consciousness. The idealists just could not stomach the thought that consciousness was not much more than a fancy lump of clay, differing not at heart from rocks, tables, and dirt; thus, they were always on hand with the question 'but where does the impression of matter have its existence?'. The answer, of course, is that material impressions exist only in consciousness, and so the conclusion is obvious; all matter is but a mental idea. This, however, was too much for the materialists, who would reply 'well the, where does consciousness come from?' The answer here being from nothing but physical processes in the human brain...and so the opposite conclusion was equally obvious; all ideas are just material. Emotions were high for both sides of the argument which could be put with equal persuasion." [5]

Heidegger thought, and I am convinced that "being-in-the-world", is an indissoluble unity constituted of what he would call existentalia (ontological details). Terms such as spatiality, temporality, and understanding or liveliness are fundamental for any possible life-world. All such existentalia are mutually implicated and equi-primordial with the others in their constitutive function with respect to the life-world. I would add ungardedness and affirmation to the essential features of human existence (life-world) as well; but more about that later.

Because of the either-or confusion about reality, physicists have reached what is called an "annihilating edge". They have had to admit that the assumption that an observer is somehow separate from the events observed has proved untenable. Inexplicably perhaps, subject and object have, ultimately, become so intimately united in our thinking that the theories that assumed otherwise now lay in ruin. The world may be called physical or mental, as one pleases but, as Bertrand Russell summed it up these words serve no purpose. However, as quantum physics reveals, all events are actually only tendencies to exist ("sourced" probability waves rippling across a dimensionless present), the "observer" plays an important role in determining what is most likely to occur (a functional "participant" during measurement/observation).

The quantum mechanical view discovered that matter seems indefinite (at a basic level) relative to the experimental situation, and seems to behave as if it were spread out infinitely. It is this strange state of unpredictability and non-locality that refers us to so-called "unstructured consciousness" (coherent episodes that makes up "awareness"). Ms. Zohar asks us to consider awareness, at a primary level, a functional phase within a living medium. The author puts her case as follows.

"The system first described by Professor Herber Frohlich of Liverpool University, some twenty years ago, and known to exist in biological tissue, seems to satisfy all the necessary criteria. Frohlich's 'pumped system' is simply a system of vibrating, electrically charged molecules (found in the cell walls of living tissue) into which energy is pumped. As they jiggle, the vibrating molecules emit electromagnetic vibrations just like so many miniature radio transmitters. Frohlich demonstrated that beyond a certain threshold any additional energy pumped into the system causes its molecules to vibrate in unison. They do so increasingly, until they pull themselves into the most ordered [condensed] phase possible – a so-called Bose-Einstein condensate. The crucial distinguishing feature of Bose-Einstein condensates is that the many parts that go to make up an ordered system not only behave as a whole, they become a whole; their identities merge or overlap in such a way that they lose their individuality entirely. A good analogy would be the many voices in a choir, which merge to become one voice at certain levels of harmony." [5]

Kaftos and Nadeau are convinced, much like Zohar, that the dynamic neuronal patterns generated by the brain are the basis for our representations of reality, and they have enfolded within themselves the previous stages/ states of/in the life of the cosmos. They argue that, in the grand interplay of quanta and fields (in whatever stage of complexity) including the very activities of our brains, there is literally nothing that can be presumed isolated or discrete. They assume we can infer that human consciousness participates in the interrelated 'conscious universe' it describes. Therefore, in their opinion, notions of an 'alienated' mind, no matter how real feelings of dissociation might be in psychological terms, are not in accord with scientific facts. (<u>The Conscious Universe</u>, Springer-Verlag, 1990).[12]

This "self-song" is a new idea, involving properties and qualities not exclusively possessed by constituent "voices". In this proposal, Mind "sings" a bio-dynamic "score" for the nervous system to "read". Each tone (conscious phase) played is blended, "musically", over time, on this view, by overlapping and modulation making future wavelengths harmonic with past to achieve coherent "mind".

Ultimately, we are challenged to accept a wedding of physics and psychology (a new model of how consciousness works). Of course, we have been warned that circumspect thinkers wisely restrain themselves from the temptation of eclecticism. The proposed view could also require a new conceptual language of the kind many thinkers would be quite fond.

Zohar concludes that: "Like particle systems, our selves are partially integrated systems of sub-selves that, from time to time, assert their own 'identities'. Their boundaries shift and merge as the patterns within the relational whole shifts… we are at times more fragmented and at times more 'together'. And, the strength of the Self, at any moment, the amount of awareness and attention that 'I' can bring to bear on my-self, my environment, or my relationship to others, depends entirely upon the extent to which my sub-selves are integrated at that moment. 'I' am an ever-present witness to the dialog between my 'selves', 'I' am the highest unity of all my many sub-unities."[5] Because of the proposed quantum mechanical qualities of this bionomic whole, as she sees it, the composite "I"

she would posit is not no-thing, it is not an illusion. "…
admittedly, it can never be reduced to a mere collection
of separate selves nor to a collection of separate brain
states. 'I' am not my rebellious self or my conventional
personality; both are aspects of me… nor am 'I' the various
brain events tht give rise to jiggling in the molecules of
my neuron cell walls. Quantum systems can't be reduced
in that way. The unity of the quantum self is a substantial
unity a thing in-itself that exists in its own right."[5]

I can't argue against the possibilities posed here. But, I
hesitate to recommend commitment to this line of reasoning
because there is only feeble correspondence between
compositions well-tuned for life's quantum-conscious
choir (sentience), and, I imagine, the programmatic score
writ for subtle personkinds of instruments to sing.

PARENTHETICALLY ...

I'm convinced that my simple investigation has managed to maintain the intercurrence of "*self*" with other objects recognized, somewhat, over time. How much any sequence of occurrences might be taken for some coherent (memorable) sort of thing or event, I've found, depends on how much it matters. That is, in truth, we must accept responsibility for the 'emergence' of life-time/world and for the 'unfolding' of reality (in a lifetime). Actual stuff, it seems, operates peculiarly (for-*oneself*) in ideation, and no reductional refuge awaits to which such things might somehow fly away from their knower's sight.[2]

I've tried to cleverly avoid the realist errors of assuming that "knowing" is merely perception (or just reception) of reality. I also hope to have quieted any idealist worry that the same "knowing" (thought-about stuff) can't assume different intuitive guises (have ontic modes) or make the phenomenological leap, for us, from one operational orbit to another. [4]

Scientifically speaking; I'm told there can be no absolute order of "things" immune from formal contingency (or, at best, just a $_{10}10^{123}$ fraction of some holo-physical "absolute" that is imaginable at any given time). Moreover, we are told that coherent actuality is an alternating current of probability (waves of ideas) through which thought wades. In the bionomic pools and eddies of quantum-reality consciousness ("I am"), one might well imagine, gurgles like a vacuous froth. But, I find no easy footing, for myself, in the muddy mysteries of modern biology. To my ear, no solo voice hums cradlesong's melody above the pulsing bass strain of simple life here. [5]

While basic science has purchased solemnity with its radical impersonality (not surprisingly), it is self-awareness that occupies our essential concerns and waking wants. Psychological investigation has managed to uncover nodal moments of awakening when *person*-being hangs unworn or unminded, and I suggest that thinking, perhaps, stitches selfsame *persons* together thwartwise, along the warp of lapsing memory and weft of reflexive attention, embroidering life's fabric; as it should now be obvious I'm interested in unraveling. [1]

I do have an inescapably intimate acquaintance with the meaning of *person* used in common discourse among my familiars and contemporaries; which helps me find where "I" might rest content. And, here I must thank the reader for following my rambling conversation thus far. [3]

One last note here about *person*'s (proper) workings in philosophical talk.

"... in speech, self-consciousness, qua independent separate individuality, comes as such into existence so that it exists <u>for others</u>. The 'I' that utters itself is heard or perceived... expressed more definitely it raises the individuality, which otherwise is only presumed existence, into the existence of its pure form... for it is in the name alone that the difference of the individual from everyone else is not only presumed but is made actual <u>by all</u>. In he name, individual counts as pure individual, no longer only in his own consciousness but in the consciousness of everyone." (<u>Phenomenology of Spirit</u>, G.W.F. Hegel, AV Miller, Oxford U Press, 1977)[11]

I have, admittedly, not yet discovered how "sociality" (conscience) or moral sense (virtue) fit into the ontological gap where I find myself now put. Conscientious "frames of mind" mark occasions when, I presume, our attention turns toward other-persons. If my private *person–being* fails to contend with some distinctly **other**-*person*(s) then, I fear, the very meaning of individualization could break down for one-self and a horrible, empty solipsism remain. Conscience, by my definition, also points toward an ideal common "humanity" (for which I will now search).

There is, of course, a great deal of controversy about whether *social* means anything at all. Nevertheless, the meta-persona idea, per se, has found many devious fissures scarring the very bedrock of scientific rigor through which it leaks into philosophic discussion (as the following demonstrates).

"Virtually all contemporary models of *social* reality invoke atomized units (persons) which are assumed to interact with one another in terms of laws or forces external to themselves. These laws or forces, it is supposed, thereby influence the units to form systems, which are themselves isolated from other such systems. The same sorts of laws or forces are then supposed to act externally on these isolated organizations to form closed megasystems. The sum of all this is finally taken to be the social whole." (<u>Conscious Universe</u>, Kafatos Nadeau, Springer-Verlag pub.)[12]

One might try to describe social facts only as particular assortments of stuff, not very formally organized and, having no clearly defined parameters or aim, depending very largely on subjective criteria. This is often considered unsatisfactory, if I'm not mistaken, because the extreme individualist or nominalist refuses, therefore, to grant whatever is *social* any substantial reality. Opponents of "social science" consider it an illegitimate pursuit because, they maintain, so-called *social wholes* (life-worlds) are imaginary constructs which should be avoided. Miller, who cites the arguments of Fichte, Schelling, Howison and Royce in rebuttal, thinks that reality only appears in *social* context and that "the communal status of nature, often invoked by realists, expresses the union of minds and has no meaning apart from them, nor they from nature". [6b]

COMMON SENSE

I think that I can find a more (or less) oblique route to social ideas through the writings of serious authorities, like Hastorf & Cantril[13] who've decided that, within any matrix of occurrences likely to be transpiring, no event becomes 'experiential' (memorable) until some *social* significance is given to them (as an aspect of what makes them important enough to think about). We're caught persistently reenacting a "social world" which we then take for granted (with all of the "personal" thoughts, feelings and behaviors that keep it going) over time, I'd say.

Also guilty of indulging the idea of *social* selves are Peter Berger and Thomas Luckmann, who wrote the following: "This [segment] is the truly 'social self ... my relevance structures intersect with the relevance structures of others at many points, as a result of which we have interesting things to say to each other ... an important element of my knowledge of everyday life is the knowledge of the relevance structures of others."[14]

Some *social* connivances, such as Berger & Luckmann construct, involve habits of mind that eventually solidify into conventions tempering our daily conduct (and working within social-lifetimes, I assume, to resolve inescapable moral quandaries), and which we need to communicate about.

I think that each of us is aware that the swells of social-lifetime into which we must dive are tidal. Fortunately, inter-personal inlets (culture, crowd, or family) are dialogical 'safe harbors', so to speak, where one's ambition to swim may be indulged (buoyed or sunk). It does seem that our intentions flounder in the shallows of dispute, misconception or misinformation while, otherwise, we might float surfeited in the current/flow of sociality. There may be surges and ebbs of "common knowledge"; as with that suggested by the analysis of Joseph J. Schwab, who suggests that *social* attitudes are not merely indexical or addable knowledge but, and I think more importantly, perpetually deliberative matters.

"… (a) each member interacts with others gives and receives approbations and criticisms, learns to know one another; (b) individual contributions to deliberation and choice are memorialized, appealed to in the course of subsequent discussion and made a matter of record; (c) the sequence of problems dealt with by the group have connections with one another; (d) the successive contributions of each individual are themselves objects of discussion and critical attention".[15]

The cultural heritage with which I deliberately "identify" is African-American and, unfortunately, my progenitors were held as chattel slaves and dismissed from common kindness. Currently we have been demonstrably deprived of civil rights, woefully disadvantaged and often discriminated against. Poverty now runs rife among us and our aspirations remain spitefully blunted. I was obliged to swim against the prevailing social tide with the rebellious defiance and prideful pique that displayed bravery in my youth. I was among many insubordinate "spokespersons" who insisted that justice prevail for the downtrodden, opportunity be made available for the impoverished, and rightful safeguards established for the most vulnerable. My public *identity* required a proud spokes-personality, and it may be the case that there are those who are just as outspoken about other things (such as G.H. Mead suggests) with which they 'identify'.

Tellhard de Chardin also reminds us that we are mostly similar sorts of persons, when he writes: "regardless of the person I approach, provided the same flame of expectation burns in us both, there is a profound, definitive and total contact instantly established between us. We feel that we are of the same kind, and we find that our very differences are a common armour, as though there were a dimension of life in which all striving makes for nearness, not only within a public body but heart to heart".

There are alternative dispositions, contrary to mine of course, inclined to see dark skinned citizen's deprivations and disadvantages as having been mostly relieved (assuming that their disfavor and despair, spanning centuries, no longer invokes serious concern nor commands somber worry) and that my presumptions as outworn.

Perhaps any *common stock* of knowledge must be re-learned, restored and/or replenished over time, to avoid conflict. I think that *conscience* can be 'reassured' somewhat within a cloudy dialogical recollection. And, although lifetime may seem ready-made, it is reconsideration, restoration and commemoration that are always at play, as we go along.

I will be careful here to avoid presenting lifetime as absorbing us in a homologous "spirit", as such notions are unimaginable for skeptics who can't muster the cosmic religious feelings that mystified Einstein or are too cynical to have confidence in quaint romantic notions like "common spirit". Fear not, however, for I'm confident that autonomous self-determination is not some illusion and that no theosophical force field is required to protect personal privacy.

Some "Pieces of the Conversation" we are having, as Michael Schwalbe calls it, may get more puzzling with regard to "sociological mindfulness" of the kind I have been after (trying to gauge the intertwining ends of sentiment, or reckon personkinds beyond oneself). Mindfulness as a sociological process, as I'll have it, can be dialogically construed as transmitted in the form of councils and lessons that convey, express or merely intimate (heart to heart) how "lifetime" is appropriately lived (or can be represented in ritual, artcraft, or cultural mannerisms/idiosyncrasies). Durkheim thought about a stock of 'social knowledge' featuring a *dialogicality* of consciousness (what I'd call 'conscience') that I obviously find interesting.

Cummings studied how various representations, whether 'public' and 'private', are formed in 'the mind', and found that important representation can be taken up, as models that are recognized (socially) and definitions in which we have confidence. If we agree with his analysis, I can imagine a formal model of 'sociality' without which the definition of one-self is lost.

I'm afraid that previously acceptable psychological theories have discounted the peculiar integration of 'personal' and 'social'. I'm not surprised, however, to find much of current social psychology pondering "interaction", "inter-subjectivity", "assimilation" and "exchange", which touch upon that ignorance. The writing of Ivana Markova[18] is particularly enlightening in this regard when she proposes that "different kinds of *social knowledge* co-exist **in** discourse and in "common sense".

I'd argue that there are dialogical components of personkindness that we can recognize and, I think, it is through discourse itself that the socio-emotional 'conscience' (from within a stock of "social" knowledge) develops as it divulges self-conscious expressions/representations of temperament ('individual' character) over lifet-ime.

EMOTIONALLY INVOLVED ...

By the way, although I'm not knowledgeable about the neuroscience nor neuro-psychology of sensation; while private consciousness may have a "feeling" (immediate sense), I argue that "emotion" is a societal construct, requiring a stock of social knowledge about the meaning of feelings (good, bad or just trying). I think that knowing how much of which sort of energy (feeling) is imbued in social life-time/world events does matter very much to us. And, I'm convinced that, within lifetime reckoning, twitching nerves will move the appropriate 'societal' muscles (when wanting is strong enough), and then we're moved to act *personally*. But, even when conscience is indecisively transmitted (modulating erratically between expectation and history, if you will), I think one must, nevertheless, constantly reset their attitude and leap naively forward.

The space for acting rightly can shrink (when we feel hurried) or widen too far (where we become disoriented) when powerful feelings compel our attention, for instance, or when the feelings of others oblige our indulgence. Operating at various sociological levels (such as familial or cultural), one can manage to act in the interstitial spaces where we find ourselves encumbered by a fretful or desperate disposition.

Of course, although the masking of strong feelings, or not feeling yet, is an 'acting' skill at which I've become adept, once unmasked, emotions are sociologically refined from raw feeling, I argue. Let me offer the following formula for your consideration. Beginning when Feeling's Intensity (at $_T$ime 1) is modified by Experience and Dialogue, I think then it is that Sentiment (and its appropriate Urgency or our worry about it) can be Manufactured (fashioned) with sufficient Aggregation (transmission); yielding the familiar socio-emotional Priorities we accept as guides – or more *M*achiavellian operations might unexpectedly follow.

$$[(FI_{T1} \div E\&D) > (S\&U \div MA)] = P_{T1} \text{ v } [(FI_{T1} \div E\&D) > (S\&U \div A)] = PM_{T2}.$$

We must carefully consider how our societal priorities might be deceitfully manipulated, I would warn (as I'm sure Chomsky would). I'm sure socio-emotional "response time" for possible behavior also has its functional rewards, so we remain wisely adverse to appalling situational options (inefficient reticence, for instance). However, when it happens that what might be done is hazardous or reckless, but inaction is just as perilous, then we stand confused and vulnerable to malevolent influences or impressed by nonsense. But, we try pushing emotional buttons or pulling back on sticky sociological throttles, nevertheless, just to get along.

Americans, for instance, it is assumed are driven by 'progressive optimism'. And, I stubbornly insist that our potential remains undiminished (to build a Great Society or explore a New Frontier). But, it is feared that we have now become too de-moralized (in the sense of losing ethical integrity) and that we lack the honest discernment or good judgment we once had. The reason for this, I imagine, is that 'social' intentions are too ill-defined or complicated to adequately prick one's conscience or ignite one's 'social' activism.

Sociologist Charles Horton Cooley (1902), by the way, introduced the rather uncomfortable idea of "looking-glass self" to suggest that we inter-subjectively "mirror" each other. Expanding on that, George Herbert Mead (1934) insisted that we come to know ourselves mostly by imagining how another perceives us and then we incorporate those perceptions into the heart of our selves (our "identities"). Using this logic, after some reflection I should be able to roughly forecast or anticipate how another might/should be expected to behave (in the mirror of imagination), but I remain poorly equipped to meet providence and unsure about what another will do. Human being, I must admit, is a deeply wayward mental process that I'm seldom able to completely recollect, reconstruct or predict, but I keep trying.

Just between us, any common emotional state might, admittedly, only result in private befuddlement or simply get forgot too quick to matter, I fear. Moreover, as Schwalbe warns, "when it seems like life is a race, few people may want to stop to analyze what all the racing is about or where it is leading, lest they fall behind."[19]

However, some thinkers must inevitably re-investigate themselves, to determine how they've actually been moved (or stumbled) through life, and then recall what was the conscious 'oomph' (of living agency) accompanying them – that is, I must resolve how it felt to have done something about which I can then be held responsible (responsible for the feeling as much as the doing), and I will pursue this idea later.

I also think that we have a "thick" experience (feeling) of ourselves as *agent-causes* that goes beyond any particular doing. Regarding the exercise of human agency, philosophers have suggested that an agent acts on any desire with which they are "satisfied" (where satisfaction is a state of absence of alternative inclinations). Daniel Wegner worries, on the other hand, that what we decide to do is based on what the "strongest desire" we have demands. And, he would have us dismiss facetious insubordination (such as I might sometimes try to ignore the influence of inconvenient urges and irks).

ENLIVENED...

I'm convinced that, among the perspectival constructs of personkinds we must include individual "potency" (agency) as an important element. Further, it may be the case that the feeling of agency can be considered a background effect of inhabited life-time. Of course, I assume that what 'volition' has come to mean for my contemporaries is merely potency/capacity and energy/effect. Any satisfactory interpolations of the proper meaning of 'action' (or sorts of reasons for doing) it is assumed philosophy will gladly provide. Considering willing and motivation, I fear, puts us at the very heart of the 'functioning' of consciousness. What is "to be done" (pragma) and/or what I think is "within my power to do" (potency) must be discovered/disclosed as life-timed measurements. Willing seems to me to be a "poetic" exercise, I'd say.

Aristotle limited will to the means by which saying "yes" to Being is accomplished. Although the Cartesian answer (Descartes) does not suffer from the Aristotelian drawback, because it got rid of the distinction between ways and endings, it, nevertheless, could not help us determine the necessary relationship between the two powers/faculties of willing and wanting. Kant thought the problem was fundamentally about deciding between psychology and cosmology (that is, between 'free' and 'natural' causality). Ricoeur said that "....the antinomic structure of a philosophy of will, as with Aristotelian, Augustinian and Cartesian descriptions, led to a sort of breaking-point...Now that nature is considered as a regular succession of phenomena, there is no longer any place within nature for an absolute power of choosing. The idea of an absolute beginning can no longer be a cosmological idea", and I'm convinced of the same (now).

I return to John William Miller's work for clarity here. I think he rightly concludes; "The individual (and so action and motive) is not discovered as some unconnected absolute. Motive and intent do not appear in any present that owes nothing to its past. Why say this? Because it is often supposed that an event not in the order of anonymous nature could be only an abrupt and unordered event an anarchic event. Action, then, has suggested a repudiation of order, at most an alleged interference with the order of nature and, in some cases, with the control and order of the supernatural. At worst, the alleged action and motive are nonsense, not even interference. Science and action do have in common that neither deals in abrupt catastrophe. Each presents a continuum. Motives and intentions get identified in a continuity of action. Science itself collapses where measuring, counting, reasoning, handling, looking, and so forth do not embody and have not embodied a continuum of action. If no verb, then no science and scientist. And, if no past tense – as previous saying doing, inquiring – then no science." (6a)

Honoria Wells, a so-called "introspectionist", through experiments concerning motivation discovered that: "when subjects are not theorizing about how deliberation and decision-making occur, they describe the process in relatively passive terms: subjects were aware of a need to choose, of various desires and thoughts coming to mind and of these desires and thoughts leading to a decision".28 Introspectionists, like her, found what they called "volition", but said little about the experience of deliberating or choosing. Wells' test subjects did not use the terms 'consciousness of action' or refer to 'the self' in her studies. They did, however, report about what they identified as 'being immediately caught in the experience of self-activity'.

I find it frustrating, as do Nahmias, Morris, Nadelhoffer and Turner20, that studies about free choice, deliberation, and voluntary action, have focused on supposed "objective conditions" for decision-making, but not on the experience of volition (for-oneself), as I would want to do. The so-called 'responsible subject' must consider the question of motivation and distinguish between duress and preference, I've decided. As Ricoeur puts it, "will is the alternative between yes and no; in that sense it is a kind of absolute; even divine freedom has no greater extension; it simply consists in the power of doing something or not doing it, in the power of affirmation and negation and in itself this power has no degrees; there are only degrees of clearness in our motives and reason, not in the power of contraries."

Whether "choice" has to do with practical logic - what Aristotle called, the logic of natural causation (a natural cause is that without which one could not act) - the "preferences" of agents are activated, I'd assume, when imagination ignites insight and lights up the improbable, so to speak. For Augustine, it is interesting to remember, the human 'will' is just the power to say "no", negate what is true, or even to deny 'Being' itself.

The maddeningly furtive forces enlivening life-time, such as volition, are on some accounts, thought to be both sensible and cerebral at each moment (simultaneously), or both meaningful and measurable, if you will. I've seen that one concocts a self-concept with introspection and expresses it (dialogically), and must maintain a stable sense of personkindness for one-self (practically). Recognizing this, I've managed to satisfy my own disposition to promote the importance of psycho-social sentiments, discourse and ontological conjecture - while neglecting much of the 'hard science' of quantum-conscious processes and carefully bypassing the alchemy of modern neuroscience, I'm afraid. I will continue to concentrate on the dialogical meaning of life-time (world) and how/why I will act in it.

The term *elan vital* (Bergson, Time and Free Will, 1889), or vital life, is an interesting description of the thread of experience one must follow or, alternatively, there is the term *erlebnis* (Wilhelm Dilthey) which can be used to refer to the confusing notion of 'lifetime'. Both terms are meant to be clearly distinguished from 'pure experience' (or what Kant called Erfahrung). But, I find the term *vivencia* (a truncation of convivencia, meaning conviviality that Jose Ortega y Gasset used) conveys the 'liveliness' of epistemic events more eloquently. Although each episode of life-time/world is suitable, so to speak, for its own reasons, I think, what my duty demands is simply to find a comfortable place for myself where I can ease the worries, disappointments or dissonance of lifetime, as a rule, and avoid interference suffered or given.

Evidently...

1. Liveliness persists throughout life-world (if seemingly intermittent)

    a. there are functional leaps of coherent apperception 'moving' from life-world mode to mode

    b. sense/feeling and socio-emotional sensibility (conscience) enliven life-time for-oneself

    c. the vital oomph of cognitive acts (thinking/doing) in life-world is idiosyncratic (personal/private)

2. 'Frames of mind' are conscious horizons found/ available in life-world, but never 'perceived' or presented by any particular cognitive act

    a. reflection and introspection are self-revealing ('self-conscious') frames of mind

    b. stocks of common knowledge and socio-emotional sentiments/dispositions emerge, viz dialogic engagement of personkinds, in life-world.

3. We have a "thick" experience of ourselves as agent-causes, having potency/volition that flares and disappears, and takes time to go from surging to fading over lifetime.

a. Alexander Pfander (Phenomenology of Willing, 1900) insists that willing is not a passive sequence of events or inertial unfolding of the mind.

i. Each act of willing feels like an abrupt force, happening 'suddenly' transposing the course of action and perception (a leap).

b. Psychological urgency (want) and socio-emotional priority (need) are maintained unsteadily between past and future temperament (where, I imagine, decision-making succeeds or fails)

Authors writing about human lifetimes usually aim to achieve a sound understanding of the sphere of so-called "authentic" acts of consciousness; as Freud did when he tried to discover them through an archeology of desire (Ursprung of consciousness) and Hegel attempted to reveal with a teleology of the spirit (telos of knowing). Nevertheless, both Hegel and Freud see language itself as the mediator between Ursprung and telos. But, what to do and why must still be "decided" somehow.

FOR GOOD REASON...

If we are 'entangled' with existence and can influence (or, at least, enliven) events across space-time by dint of willing – perhaps just bumbling around without predictable consequences – then our imaginary (socio-intuitive) schemes and inventive (experimental) sciences may not be merely vain pursuits. Ultimately, I insist that 'being' is unremittingly challenging and that: "what characterizes the free man is his capacity and determination to make 'history'. It is not any static truth that can make men free. In that static guise the truth only enslaves. It is rather in the revision of truth that freedom is found. To cease that activity, to suppose there is any termination of care and labor, is to entertain an illusion and to relapse into a dream." (6b) More, we might even happen upon a convenient ethical principle or divine situation without fear of retribution.

I am usually confident about representing myself as a rational, purposive entity who has fit my cognizance to what I want to do (or need to know) and how. I interpret what I might do in terms of *reasons* for which I will act or have acted (involving intentions, purposes, beliefs or desires/motives). I am attentive to possible descriptions of the actions of others and of the possible reasons for them to act (as such vigilance will surely guard me against their sins).

The gist of an action can, I think, be explained by what the agent thinks or felt about doing it. The meaning of a movement or signal is often understood by reference to the kind of forthcoming action it intends (has a reason to perform or conveys). Citing a *reason* for an action serves to explain how or why the action is done. There must be modes of sentiment, assumption or purposes that, I'd assume, involve reasons for action. I'm sure there are categories of such reasons (such as dispositional, mechanical, or logical for instance) that can be used to describe tendencies or describe purposes for acts. Many intentions or motives can play a role in any action that operates to produce actions, I think. We, ourselves, are thought to willingly undertake all of this, a priori, of course.

In 'pure' science we try to eliminate reference to dispositions and purposes (what may well be) in favor of theoretical 'certainty' about the properties of objects. Descriptions of the events which trigger an action must, of course, involve the objective attributes that must be integrated into any formulae that 'covers' actions. However, in the description of that action we also cite motivations and dispositions for it to emerge from clouds of reasons which can be traced through in many ways, just as well.

I don't deny that we have trouble forming any rules connecting purpose to action; neither by specifying the conditions in which the disposition to act can be manifested nor by predicting the conditions under which any agent (with a disposition) will act. It may be beyond our capability, surely beyond mine I fear, to strengthen our predictive capability in this regard, and we must accept that descriptions of acts, regardless of prevailing conditions, will remain logically undependable or incomplete.

What I try to keep clear, here, is that we do depict each another in a way that entails having cogent *reasons* to act (over time) and, in this same sense, we make a general prediction about any action that there will be evidence of such *reasons* to be found. Thereby we explain what has been done or is likely to be done by someone.

James Hopkins tries to clear our thinking about '*reasons*' thusly: "We can regard ourselves as taking each descriptive explanation as liable to confirmation or disconfirmation through coherence or dissonance with other explanations of the same kind…Where the desires and beliefs in one explanation cohere and overlap with those of others, the explanations are mutually confirming. Since explanations by *reasons* are thus either confirmed or disconfirmed by relation to others, giving the best account of an agent's actions requires fitting the pattern of his actions to the pattern of his motives [as explained] as a whole, so as to achieve the greatest coherence".[22] This kind of verification/falsification of overlapping *reasons* (in the explanation of any desire or motivation to act), giving an account of 'belief' or 'disposition', Hopkins thinks, can be compared to the statistical testing of hypotheses, but I wouldn't bet on that.

'Yet to be determined', of course, is the conditional quality I want to reserve for self-conscious action (retained only for me, personally, in a sense) that will separate my doing from knowing – although neither witlessness or disinterest are excuses if actions are to have meaning at all. I fear that my own reasons for undertaking this study, for example, might prove methodologically fragmentary, distorted or just barely measurable at this point - in which case any ingenious insight remains unlikely, but, I go on. I'm convinced that no amount of inference about what is likely or survey of prevailing conditions will satisfactorily explain my actions. Nevertheless, I wake, plan and persevere, for the best reasons I can follow, regardless of what the case may be. I will do what I 'must', and I will accept *personal* responsibility for my actions (regardless of my reflective honesty) and for the scatterbrained rationalizations I often make for what I've done. I reconstruct which reasons will explain some act best only when disposed to notice the significance of some situation in which I was in some way obliged to act. Decisions to act, I conclude, can be best explained in such terms of reflective consciousness.

The philosophical questions remain; "what is my personal responsibility", and "why/how do I undertake its accomplishment (for what reason must I care to?).

It is clear to me that, although physical science might be able to determine how "thinking" is done and, perhaps, what "thoughts" are, science can't decide which thoughts we will have before us (or when we should have them), however likely some thinking may eventually be.

Insufficiencies of eidetic memory, as much as differences (relativity) of life-time/space perspective make conjecture as regards common conscience even more confusing, I'm afraid. If there is no way to verify whether why/what whatever we do answers to some logic or nous then, perhaps, it's the case that 'conscience' is only a contractual/incidental convenience (or license) that is roughly considered 'rightful' or generally consistent with ordinary well-being (however insufficient that may be for some religious reasons).

Hegel poses the problem thusly: "From this point of view, no immanent doctrine of duties is possible; of course, material may be brought in from outside and particular duties may be arrived at accordingly, but if the definition of duty is taken to be the absence of contradiction then no transition is possible to the specification of particular duties nor, if some such particular content for acting comes under consideration, is there any criterion in that principle for deciding whether it is or is not a duty.

A dubious notion that I would carefully avoid here is that third-personal "objectivity" will suffice for dutiful behavior (or give good reason to act). A third-person viewpoint is not, I think, just as suitable (satisfactory) as those reasons discovered from first-person standing. As has been observed before, this idea presents a problem of "dissociation", about which foregoing wisdom has been wary. For so-called "agent neutral" reasons to be found (for anyone), these must be considered 'objectified' in order then to become "possessed" by someone (no matter whom), and that "moral" perspective, it's decided, turns out to be just someone's 'private take' on an inter-subjective sum. It must then be admitted that any person's standpoint can legitimately cap the demands placed on it, rendering any agent-neutral reasons impotent.

Randall offers the following way out. He shows how socio-emotional images (symbols embedded in religious language) can stir people to feel, strengthen their commitment, and foster action, through common (cooperative) responses to those imageries. He develops an 'aesthetic' explanation for this that refers to the poet's words, the painter's colors or the musician's notes. He writes: "Poetic symbols show us how to discern unsuspected qualities in the world encountered, latent powers and possibilities there resident. Still more, they make us see the new qualities with which the world, in cooperation with the spirit, can clothe itself...They teach us how to see what man's life in the world is, and what it might be. They teach us how to discern what human nature can make out of its natural conditions and materials...They enable us to see and feel the religious dimension of our world better, the order of splendor, and of man's experience in and with it."[30] Of course, even purely "poetic" symbolic forms can deteriorate when inactive, and can oscillate on many conjectural registers.

I suspect psycho-social sentiments (conscience) are somehow projected onto lifetime, as traces (signs) of imperfect personkindness in one's doings. I wonder whether one reconstructs 'antecedent' moral reasoning - essentially, when there's no longer immediate awareness of motives (if there ever was) or need to explain acts. The difficulty, then, is how to explain what has been added to, superimposed on, or substituted in "immediate" understanding of what might be meant (over time).

I'd question whether any psycho-social state (willing or no) is more than a vague, non-cognitive field where personkindness blindly operates. There may, however, be some reason to distinguish between agent-relative pleasures and some inevitable, agent-neutral duty (displeasure?) for us to consider. I'm also curious whether "doing-good" happens only in that space where socio-emotional symbols would belong or belongs somewhere else? I'm not even certain whether moral uprightness is proper to "religious" assertions alone, but I'm hard pressed to decide why it shouldn't be.

Nonetheless, conscience settles into its proper place, I'm convinced, where the important thing is agent-relative introspection – when even a simple act of kindness is involved. I'm convinced that compassion is the rule, rather than the exception, that we follow and that any lifetime/space requires both magnanimity (openness) and conviviality (conscience) to operate, for 'good' reason. Although the only personal responsibility one has, I fear, may be to rightly 'fulfill' the responsibility to 'maintain' one's life-time/space well, and to honestly negotiate each conciliatory treaty of conscience (make up one's mind), we must also measure our influence on other's lives (within the bounds of socio-emotional life-time/space).

When Christine Korsgaard searched carefully through the history of thought to find the force of moral "obligation", she found that the so-called 'rational intuitionism' of the early eighteenth century (which looked for intrinsic normative properties of values and obligations existing objectively) was supportive of moral claims regardless of perspective. But, later, as she observes, it was decided that human nature itself is the source of morality (especially when we ask the 'normative question' about whether there are important reasons to "be good"). Korsgaard eventually decides that moral obligation is self-imposed, giving us final authority over ourselves, for which conclusion she has been accused of Kantianism. Her argument is that, since self-consciousness is essentially reflective, reflexivity can generate feelings of resentment when our deeds are thought to be immoral or wrong.

On this view, values are "projections" of fearful sentiments and dispositions onto the world. She writes: "our capacity to turn our attention onto our own mental activities is also a capacity to distance ourselves from them, and to call them into question. I perceive, and I find myself with a powerful impulse to believe? But, I back up and bring that impulse into view and then I have a certain distance. Now the impulse doesn't dominate me and now I have a problem. Shall I believe? I desire and I find myself with a powerful impulse to act. But, I back up and bring that impulse into view and then I have a certain distance. Now the impulse doesn't dominate me and now I have a problem. Shall I act? Is this desire really a reason to act? The reflective mind cannot settle for perception and desire, not just as such. It needs a reason. Otherwise, at least as long as it reflects, it cannot commit itself or go forward."[17]

By this reasoning I'd have to consider all versions of morality "true", and must think "normativity" will spring from some legislative authority we command over manifestation of ourselves – to compel obedience and punish disobedience, according to the rules (reasons) we obey or decide (for some reason) to defend.

By the way, I find very disturbing any argument proposing that one must be determined to intend only foreseeable consequences of one's voluntary actions. As for me, it does not make any difference to someone's responsibility for any effect, even of 'foreseeable' action, if they merely have not intended only that particular effect. I think we can reject moral duty reduced to "utilitarian consequentialism" and consider alternative arguments - such as the assumption that we merely use language to perform various provisional conciliations by which we can then, valiantly, conduct our daily affairs ('braving' or confronting circumstances), perhaps.

I find human conscience (as Fromm sometime termed con-scientia) is a kind of knowledge, within oneself, about successes or failures at living life well. This assessment is, I'm convinced, the essence of 'moral' experience. To quote Fromm, "Human conscience is the expression of man's self-interest and integrity...to be selfless, unhappy, resigned, discouraged, etc. is in opposition to the demands of one's conscience..."

THE FINAL FRONTIER ...

As I have noted in my meditations on modes of emergence of personkindness and thinking about ways to arrive at one-self (privately being-thought), there must be some dimension/distance (occurrence/opportunity) where and when personkinds can be manifest and enlivened. It also seems clear that looking outward upon reality is always moving backward in lifetime, at what has already happened, while intention and willing reserve space in the future. I wonder if there is also, perhaps, an intimate recess enfolded within mindful attention, somewhere, that marvelous insight might also slip, to avoid notice. I must admit that I cannot find anywhere that is "empty" space, although there may be some 'things' that haven't happened yet, nor 'anywhere' to exit from the passing present. I'm sure that strange dimensions of thinking and plausible universes of thought will appear to distract my curiosity.

The parameters of conscious comprehension, as Alvin Tofler proposes, end with what he calls three 'deep fundamentals' that I should mention here. The first fundamental, he concludes, is time – or the sequences and sorts of 'individuals'. Secondly, there is space - wherein nexuses of attributes meld and special qualities are appreciated in pure imagination. And, thirdly, there is knowledge (puzzling?). I can fathom no greater depth of cognizance beyond these. But I'm sure, as Kant would remind me, that the concept of *space* belongs to our relation to nature, not to nature itself, and is basically a condition for our scientific descriptions of reality (a priori). Relying mostly on the simple premises and deductions of the prevalent language of reasoning, one might easily overlook the "value" of these fundamental truths, I fear.

Paul Ricoeur, using hermeneutic analysis, also found that there are three fundamentals of pure imagination; the cosmic (elementary), the oneiric (iconic/feted), and the poetic (or 'marvelous') dimensions, if you prefer. He concluded that no sense of 'pure reflection' exists for-itself, but that imagination must spend itself <u>completely</u> in the act of establishing (imagining) some 'actuality' – making more life-time/space from which proposition we can find no easy escape. Building spatial experience, it would seem, to require both the architecture of pure phenomenological imagination and psycho-social (perceptional) engineering in order to make "private" space (withheld in consciousness).

Ernst Cassirer[10] insisted, that our picture of "space" does not reveal some special class of sensation which informs us regarding magnitude, position or distance but, rather, reveals a different faculty by which we recognize a "synthesis of the spirit". And, this capability, he thinks, is grounded not in the rules of abstract logic or formal mathematics but in those obeyed by the imagination. Or, as someone else said it; "All 'wheres' are disclosed and exhibited round about us through the comings and goings of everyday life, not ascertained and specified by reflective spatial measurement." And, the inference I will draw here is that "the experience of spatial form is completed only through its relation to a total horizon which it reveals to us – through a certain atmosphere in which it not merely is but in which, as it were, it lives and breathes." (Heidegger)

I would say, moreover that, between the *spatial being* built up in geometry and the fundamentally 'aspatial' being apprehended in imagination, there is no possible mediation except from the center (for-myself). The emotional exposure we risk in "poetic" space, I will offer, might strip one from the rectilinear edgings of *real-time* and require reorientation of one's thinking (surely an 'imaginative exercise', I'd say). In "poetic space" one can, I'd caution, be easily caught awestruck by some unexpected splendor, bemused by some wondrous depiction, or unnerved by the wit of welcome humor. Of course, "reflection" and "imagination", generally, are not merely about some sensuous-intuitive content which we can dissect into elementary components, nor combine into an idea of 'real' space.

They are, curious emergences from the nebulous dream of life-time, I think, that flash furtively past awareness and/or offer another orientation from which one might set about knowing. Regarding imaginative space, in general, Cassirer writes, "all acts of expressing, representing and signifying are not immediately present as such, and can never become visible except in their achievements as a whole... They do not originally look back on themselves but look toward the work they accomplish, toward

61

orienting the being whose spiritual form they have to build up."

He continues: "… manifold meaning-groups which in turn are systematically related to one another and which by virtue of this relationship constitute the totality that we call the world of our experience…are so articulated that from each of their factors a transition is possible to the whole, because the organization of this whole is representable and represented in the whole."[10]

Objectively speaking, Merleau-Ponty thinks that, to succeed in having something interesting to say about experience one must exorcise so-called standpointless thinking. He insists that there is no perception seen 'from nowhere' that would justify the possibility of perception and consciousness must inhere in a point of view. However he decided that we must take a third-person's point of view and, further, must engage in a narrative act (dialogue) where understanding life-time/world is accomplished. I'm convinced there are relative 'distances' (such as between personkinds, which result in a simple relativity of apperception) between which any 'event' must be understood to occur over time. I must also assume that every conscious viewpoint is perspectival, and what is gained from a 'point of view' may be lost from another. On this account, each viewpoint can maintain itself only by taking up a preceding challenge and opening one-self to the insurgence of other-selves.

ANYWHERE ...

A notion of one-self as "Being-here" (or "Dasein" as Heidegger would say) somehow prior to any 'real' content that might be offered, such as Eastern concepts like zero or ineffability, I'd suggest proves sadly unconvincing in Western philosophical traditions. But, I am convinced that multiversal personkinds sail the cosmic sea, riding an organizing tide wherewith (or against which) each one must swim.

So, anyway, when the phenomenologist and physical scientist are invited to compare notes about self-conscious "reality" they should both conclude, I think, that any possible world is merely a narrative brought to mind that satisfies our search for 'order'. Furthermore, I agree with Bohr's suggestion that constructing a reality of any kind requires a logical process which, essentially, works within the framework of logical complementarity. Complimentary formulations derive their existence through oppositions, but they do not [necessarily] manifest as a firmly connected causal chain, as Kaftos and Nadeau explain. "Complementary constructs are modalities of conscious awareness which, taken together, are complete formulations, or co-equal manifestations of the content of consciousness. And, they can be apprehended as [necessarily] unified, although never defined as such, on the deepest level of consciousness."[12]

Indulge me this, if you will; I wish to register a complaint about the imaginary cosmological illustrations that use games of chess or checkers to picture the process of "real" matters. Whenever a particular cosmic placeholder replaces a corresponding piece (or reoccupies a 'space-like region') it traces a timeline of persuasion to "move" (or "play"), and a destructive propensity prevails in such a case, as well; which disturbs me.

Alternatively, I happen to enjoy the game of Go. When Go pieces are placed at the intersections of a grid drawn on a board their influence over other 'identical' structures is exerted by dint of their mere presence. Tactically, 'discrete' pieces (called stones) can be considered connected (complimentary), and the integrity of formations of stones can take on what is called 'strength' or 'life' (or coherence). Moreover, when a stone's "quantum activity", so to speak, is implicitly enfolded into the "whole board" then familiar patterns will arise (in intention, I guess) and formulas of play are somehow discovered as an "implicate order" by the shrewd observer/player.

Complete games of this sort, of course, are "strategic" problems and the sequences of placements that shape, cut, or link pieces, or meet with some other 'tactical' objective, must involve many implicit threats and possibilities (about which one is never certain). The life-worlds (games) that we imagine or regret are thus enigmatically smeared over undefined life-times.

I argue that the obdurate logical uncertainty learned by physicists seems to have eluded those philosophers who insist that all consciousness must have distinct, antecedent conditions or that choices follow a plainly causal sequence (that a linear chain of desires, reasons and acts are linked via a straightforward "deliberative" process) – as if one motivation might not activate many possible choices or many motivations activate one. I'd insist that, simply because of the capricious "cortical folding" of each particular brain (through which mindfulness is realized), if for no other reason, each self 'minds' (recollects/decides) an especial individual.

One other peculiarity that, as Kierkegaard noted, will enter into anyone's individual beginning is when death may come – so, one may worry whether they've begun something worth having started. He concluded that apprehension about the uncertainty of the extent of one's life-time is impossible to feel in generality, because 'I' cannot become (or do) something merely "in general". He further explained that one's own death is by no means something in general for-oneself (but that fact may be something of the sort for others occupying the same life-time/world). Moreover, he concludes, if the very task of a lifetime-world is to become subjective, then every subject will, for themselves, be the very opposite of something in general (ie. be individual).

Sartre, who wrote brilliantly about self-consciousness, viewed any life-time/world as a unique occasion in which each moment finds its rightful place (is comprehensible on the basis of past experiences but not reducible to them nor on that of predictable ones). Sartre wanted to understand how we try to live as we do, over time, and why we want to find a particular (personal) way of doing so, as do I. And, I am convinced that we can integrate many 'acts' of consciousness or occurrences into synchronic (mindful) "wholeness" – that, of course, becomes less and less definite as more closely observed.

An interesting twist, by the way, is that we normally experience life as having 'synchronism' (coherence) but not necessarily 'chronologicality' (sequence). As Hegel concluded, the volitional 'frame of mind' relies on a disposition to make one-self a member of each moment in life, or to fend for 'oneself' in lifetime.

LIKENESS ...

The improvisation of dialogical engagement is a 'refrain' in the life-time events of personkinds, I'd say, and "lifetimes', per se, as Miller insists, are 'midworlds' (involving 'functioning objects' such as bodies, instruments, devices and signs) and not simply what we happen to do… [they are] "the story of the fatality of doing itself and short of actual immediacy, or of a present with its projected totality, neither knowledge nor history can put in an appearance." He writes: "Perhaps we will learn the hard way that the price of commodity is an ordered immediacy and learn that the act, instead of being a disorderly intruder into the scientific world, is the source and support. The disorderly intruder view of the act has become an axiom of science and is quite proper on cognitive premises. Those who persist in wanting life and action are regarded as anti-intellectual, superstitious, or primitive. And, in a way they are. But, in what way? In the way that treats both present and totality as objects rather than as actualities. If act and life do not define and generate a world, they cannot be found within it. We are not even alienated on such premises; we are nullified – and any totality along with our own presence." (ibid.)

It would be easy to assume that there is 'likeness' of representation of all life-time/space among its inhabitants, and uniformity of *cooperative dialogic arrays* such that the expression of moral action (conscience) should be 'smooth' throughout it. But, experimental investigation might, just as easily, prove otherwise. 'Sociality' (conviviality, if you will), for instance, might be warped around what matters within galaxies of individuals and seem distorted for those outside that particular cluster (bending in a sort of 'gravitational arc' around the dialogical interactions formed therein). Surprisingly, putative impressions of someone's 'sociality', 'morality' or 'conscientiousness' can shatter or shift and then reform through the action of dialogical intercourse, I'd suppose.

The astronomy of social "identities", as I see it, tracks the orbital relationships, relative status and mass/potency of personkinds in a given socio-dialogic cluster (which might be considered fixed by the weight or magnitude of essential person-like traits). When deciding how to act, it might also be thought that one's own 'role', 'character' or course must be fixed in a given social life-time/space. However, if personkinds are viewed as having inexorably fixed social orbits that follow a set track over lifetime, this depiction will not satisfy the arbitrary and casual ambitions one might wish to preserve. Therefore, I expect there is relative inconsistency and nebulousness within the dialogical clusters of persons in social systems. Unfortunately, I have no metaphorical explanation for the catastrophies of psychological fracturing or breaches of 'character' of such an astronomy of personkinds as I've imagined here.

Getting back down to earth, the Social Identity theory, for which I'll search in the more familiar explanatory firmament can be of two sorts, "realistic" or "relativistic", (of which I find the latter most reasonable).

Tajfel and Turner (as found in Social Psychology, Brehm, Kassin, Fein, Hougton Co., 2005, pg. 153), claim that people strive mostly to enhance self-esteem viz personal *identity* (character) and collective approval via social identity (conviviality).

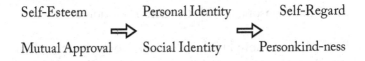

Self-Esteem	Personal Identity	Self-Regard
Mutual Approval	Social Identity	Personkind-ness

I'm convinced that, with prideful bravado, we can reach after the self-affirmation we want at every testing turn and that, regardless of constraint, condition or other shortcoming, personkinds will defy easy definition or slight regard.

Dismissive of countervailing facts, some stubborn persons maintain their independence from fate and insist upon having 'free' will. They refuse to yield control or cede 'willingness' to any formulae of neuroscience, habit or delimitation. If, for instance, physiology denies them the joy of flight they will invent a mechanical means of adding air-sickness to their lexicon of 'individual apperception'. If neurology predicts hesitation they may hurry unnervingly ahead, flouting forethought. If blinking is thought instinctual, they will stare. And, no disincentive will deter them from all such manner of vices, because willing and motivation endow personkind with an unpredictable "nature. We are able to adjust our subjective scope, in this way, and to augment or diminish tendencies to 'innately' comply with 'natural' demands.

Recent scientific experiment (when using the appropriate instruments, of course) confirms that a coherent 'group consciousness' can actually be detected, and one must ask whether personkind resonates with some *common sense* or dark psycho-social 'energy' that compels our conformity. This might lead one, therefore, to question the extent to which they can 'intend' to do anything that isn't consistent/consonant with the determination of others.

I stand here, nonplused, at a transitional epoch when the first President of African-American heritage has been elected for two terms of service. We have also been primarily occupied nowadays with recovering from terrible economic distress. However, deep-rooted social fissures and racism still scar the social horizon, and avaricious excess and irresponsibility are crevasses into which some have sadly fallen. Common purpose has been put aside and selfish gain embraced. On the other hand, I was lucky enough, as were many others, to have felt a spirit of bigheartedness during the 1960's, which I doubt has been entirely lost. The commitment of lives, fortunes and sacred honor to secure the common rights and protect the freedoms of people by mutual consent and majority rule has not been forgot. Muddled modernity and the cramp of relentless troubles we endure might anesthetize conscience, or arrest 'sociality', but I think that the obligation of the wise to undertake whatever virtuous actions one may still remains compos mentis (*common sense*).

Mind, generally, operates, I've determined, in the elements of intuition (knowing), feeling (sense), and of expression (presentation). But, is there also a socio-emotional 'conscience' which could be said to have 'miscellaneous actuality', and could it be the case that the stages of development of this 'common cognizance' are mutually exclusive from one another? Nonetheless, I think that "whatever I may claim for the satisfaction of my conviction about the character of an action as good, permitted, or forbidden ... in no way detracts from the right of objectivity [freedom]"[11], as Hegel did.

I'm convinced that explanations of mindfulness must be constructed from the inside out and that determinations or decisions imply psycho-social sentiment/disposition (as much as the having of good logical sense) where personkinds 'follow laws' for making up one's mind about tenets kept "undeniably" true.

TESTAMENT...

Ludwig Klages (Vom Wesen des Bewusstseins, 1924) took expressive experience (testament) as the Archimedean point, from which he thought we can 'lift the world of ontology off its hinges', in a way, and better understand it. He also insisted that we can "pull away from the division of being into physical and psychic". He noted; "Anyone who finds it difficult to visualize a relation which is incomparably different from that of cause and effect, and of an infinitely closer kind, need only consider the analogous relation of the sign to what it designates ... As the concept inheres in the linguistic sound so does the soul inhere in the body: the former is the meaning of the word, the latter the meaning of the body; the word is the cloak of the thought, the body is the manifestation of the soul. No more than there are wordless concepts are there souls without form."

One might ask whether we have lost our existential footing again, and slipped into mysterious ideas about abstract knowledge caught in some symbolic 'environment' which we then try to convey (with mimetic acuity, perhaps)? I'm sure the answer is no.

Dialogized heteroglossia, as Mikhail Bakhtin calls the content of discourse, is a contradiction-ridden, tension filled issue of embattled intentions trying to know about something, in lifetime (as I'd paraphrase it). This stuff, Bakhtin thinks, occupies the authentic environment of an utterance, where language takes shape. He writes: "Linguistics, stylistics and the philosophy of language that were born and shaped by the current of centralizing tendencies in the life of language have ignored this *dialogized heteroglossia*...For this very reason they could make no provision for the dialogic nature of language, which is a struggle among socio-linguistic points of view – not an intra-language struggle between individual wills or logical contradictions. Moreover, even intra-language dialogue (dramatic, rhetorical, cognitive or merely casual) has hardly been studied linguistically or stylistically up to the present day. One might even say outright that the dialogic aspect of discourse and all the phenomena connected with it have remained to the present moment beyond the ken of linguistics..."[27]

Bakhtin also notes that: "It is all the more remarkable that linguistics and the philosophy of discourse have been primarily oriented precisely toward the artificial, preconditioned status of the word, a word excised from dialogue and taken for the norm...The word is born in a dialogue as a living rejoinder within it and is shaped in dialogic interaction with an alien word that is already in the object. A word forms a concept of its own object, in a dialogic way." And, "Language – like the living environment in which the consciousness of the verbal artist lives – is never unitary. It is unitary if taken as an abstract grammatical system of normative forms in isolation from the concrete, ideological conceptualizations that fill it, and in isolation from the uninterrupted process of historical becoming that is a characteristic of all living language. Actual social life and historical becoming create within an abstractly unitary language a multitude of concrete worlds, a multitude of bounded verbal-ideological and social belief systems, and within these various systems are elements of language filled with various semantic and axiological content". (ibid)

Alexander Pfander (Phenomenology of Willing 1900, pub. 1963) helpfully describes the teeming nexuses of mental functions at the core of our dialogical engagement. He insists that such interplays of mental forces drives oneself into perspectival 'leaping' (re-setting conscious-reality from always novel angles), which I find easily conceivable, and that these leaps take place during brief spans in the ongoing movement of the mind (flare then disappear, surge then fade). But, the "movement" (extension) of such leaps may be illusory, and the tempo of that movement much like unscored jazz.

Whenever someone asks "what did you say", for instance, it's likely, I think, that they're trying to imagine what your expression/utterance divulges about the attitude (place) you will take in the curious lifetime-world about which agreement must be reached. Nevertheless, whether one takes an informative or interrogative view, it seems to me that dialogic utterances are answerable by anyone's response, although any response remains "un-disclosed" (incomplete) and always productive of further dialogical addresses and responses. Bakhtin's explanation is that: "Expropriating 'I', forcing it to submit to intentions and accents, in a difficult and complicated process...as a living, socio-ideological concrete thing, for the individual consciousness, language lies on the borderline between oneself and the other." And, "the word [utterance] is half someone else's which becomes one's 'own' only when the speaker populates it with his own intentions, his own accent, when he appropriates the word, adapting it to his own semantic and expressive intention. Prior to this moment of appropriation, the utterance does not exist in a neutral and impersonal language but, rather, it exists in other people's mouths, in other people's contexts, serving other people's intentions; it is from there that one must take the word, and make it one's own." (ibid) "Meaning", as he would have it, is, therefore, never closed for one-self, and the conceptual horizon one occupies is always oriented toward appropriation of future dialogic understanding. This dialogical life/world I occupy is immediate and incomplete, on this account, but never "impersonal", however much I might wish to look away from it.

Composers of music, and other artists, have been taught that one must learn the rules of 'form' for their art so that they will know how to break them. This is especially true in jazz music, where one is constantly expected to be creative, and analogous, I think, to dialogic interchange. Following the rules all of the time would lead to predictable and boring dialogical performances, but paying no attention whatsoever to the rules could lead, just as woefully, to boring randomness. There are many rules and conventions of both music and of discourse, but there are no criminal penalties associated with breaking musical manners, which is libel to be the case in discourse.

One can, however, experiment at new ways of communicating, and bend the rules of sophisticated dialogue which form the framework for subjecting life-time/spaces to the naming and sorting that distinguish them. The manner in which the rules of composition, depiction and expression are used will shape how well one's meaning is understood. Although the variations on a theme that the melodies of our 'individual' lives play can be more or less consonant, the talents of performers can also be more or less influential, I think. The charismatic politician or motivational speaker, for instance, can manipulate the implication and recollection of truth, for well or ill, according to their talent, and how they might break the rules of rhetoric will help define their personal style or, more importantly, their social character.

As with playing music, a verbal-ideological player needs to have a critical ear. Playing with others (dialogically), even for pure discursive enjoyment, as a conversational performer with some idea of what one is expected to say or do, you can learn, I think, to listen well. You can listen to examples of interplay and try to develop an ear for it. You can analyze dissonances and accents, to try achieve the same effects, or listen to both outbursts and whispers to expand the idea of how to best express yourself. With this talent one is less likely to be impressed with mere technical facility or good grammar, and will listen for poetic or logical sophistication. Nevertheless, if an expression reaches you emotionally then you need not worry that it does not seem particularly reasonable when scrutinized closely.

If someone misunderstands or misspeaks, and everyone else recognizes that person has erred, we can attempt to move over to match the out of place performer, although that would be difficult to coordinate if not impossible to achieve, but it is better to try to correct the person who is out of step because, ideally, you want to encourage the correct logical form. Another thing that can go wrong is an unintended time-based change when some tend to use slang or invented expressions while others tend to drag olden notions along with them. Sometimes the interaction between personkinds becomes hopelessly frustrating because it is virtually impossible to keep language- spheres synchronized (or syncopated or syntonic).

What is important to remember here is that the scope of any language-scape – that is the intentional situation in which dialogical engagement is possible - is filled with special content (symbols, senses, or events made concrete or realized) and can become permeated with "value". Within such dialogic domains, I argue, persons can express them-self well or ill, but someone outside of a given verbal-ideological purview cannot understand how/well.

Regardless of who inhabits a language-scape (horizon), finally, "at any given moment, languages of various epochs and periods of social-ideological life cohabit with one another". He gives me even more reason for confusion, I'm afraid, when he writes; "Even 'languages of the day' exist: one could say that today's and yesterday's socio-ideological and political 'day' do not, in a certain sense share the same language; every day represents another socio-ideological semantic 'state of affairs', another vocabulary, another accentual system with its own slogans, its own ways of assigning blame and praise". Moreover, "In any given historical moment of verbal-ideological life, each generation at each level has its own 'language'; moreover every age group has as a matter of fact its own 'language', its own vocabulary, its own particular accentual system that, in their turn, vary depending on social strata" (ibid.).

I suspect that, at any given moment or historical intermission, 'language-scapes' describing differing things, phases of change or expressing different sorts of thinking coincide within verbal-ideological lifecycles. Every significant verbal performance may have the ability to affect aspects of truth, for a period of time or for a sphere of personkinds, and impart some 'expressive impulse', semantic nuance and/or axiological overtone to life-time/space, in so many words. I think that life-time is lived immediately through what may be generally considered "language", and that I struggle and evolve in a dialogical environment.

Lastly: "For any individual consciousness living in it, language is not an abstract system of normative forms but a concrete conception of the world. All words have the 'taste' of a profession, a genre, a tendency, a party, a particular work, a particular person, a generation, an age group, a day and hour. Each word tastes of the contexts in which it has lived its social charged life; all words and forms are populated by intentions" and that "...language has been completely taken over, shot through with intentions and accents. As soon as a critical inter-animation of language began to occur, as soon as it became clear that these were not only various language but internally variegated, that the ideological systems and approaches to the world that were indissolubly connected with them contradicted each other and in no way could live in peace and quiet with one another – then the inviolability and predetermination of language came to an end and the necessity of actively choosing one's orientation among them began." (ibid.)

Discourse, on this account, tries to outwit itself, 'categorically' speaking. That is, for example, in political rhetoric some vague point of view will be presented to defend or protest against an allegation, contention or creed, or to proclaim a political belief toward which the utterances are 'aimed'. Discourse deals with the individual as agent through which a life-time horizon becomes as distinct as is possible and where 'allusions' can be made *meaningful* (assigned). My model of "common sense" is, in this way, framed by noises, silences, gestures and exclamations meant to reveal *social* symbols/concepts and expresses whatsoever I might feel them to imply.

Thus, language has living vitality, I think, but any dialogic relationship has limits of perspective that conceptualizes the world in words and fills it with familiar objects, meanings and values (life-time/place) from which flight is incomprehensible.

Viktor Frankl, however, has proposed a "logotherapy" of human affairs is needed to find what meaning there is in any peculiar life-time/worlds one might temporarily inhabit. He also introduced what he called a noological analysis (from the Greek noos, meaning mind/spirit) to reveal the supposed spiritual "core" of dialogical personkinds. He insists that there is a "will to meaning" there, which holds sway across and between different natures, values or viewpoints. This is different from simple drive or instinct that arbitrates 'spiritual struggle' to the pull, to and fro betwixt predicament and prediction, so to speak, in a peculiar dimension of life-time/place. Frankl admits that there may be some cases of personal worry about values that is only camouflage for hidden inner conflicts, and in such particular instances the study of the dynamics of dissociation are justified.

Furthermore, it is concluded by Frankl that: "Psychodynamic research in the field of values is legitimate ... the question is whether it is always appropriate. Above all, we must keep in mind that any exclusively psychodynamic investigation can, in principle, only reveal what is a driving force in man. But, values, however, do not drive man; they do not push him, but rather pull him... logos [spirit]," he goes on to say, "is not only an emergence from existence itself but rather, a confronting of existence. If the meaning that is waiting to be fulfilled by man were really nothing but a mere expressing of self, or no more than a projection of his wishful thinking, it would immediately lose its demanding and challenging character; it could no longer call man forth or summon him".[26]

GIST IS...

One might think that it is only when we pause to concentrate that consciousness wavers and flicks, like some elusive star in extreme orbit around one-mind's self; but no telescope will be needed for me to see where I am going from here. And, as what I call 'thought' and 'feeling' have their immediate expressions, signs and signals, what I call "mind" is an operational function (engagement) having its measurements, guesses, or reasonings about the meaning of life-time/world.

Which brings me back to John William Miller, of course, whose work so often helps dispel doubt. He writes: "No absolute is cognitive. One had better face up to that. But, if cognition be the basis for rejecting absolutes, one had better try to authorize cognition...The authorization of cognition requires an articulate immediacy, which is the actual, the verb, the counting, measuring, speaking, and much else that is entailed in any presence." (6a)

Some sort of analytic 'awakening' to the spiritual reality (logos) of one's lifetime is a fascinating idea I'd be happy to pursue, however vexing. The inadequate linguistic tools at my disposal, however, work to manipulate the meaning of things and ideas, aalthough they are all I have to work with. Optimistically speaking, Tillich has taught me that language itself can open up levels of reality which are otherwise closed to us, and he insisted that we are able to "unlock" dimensions and elements of our soul with it. (Dynamics of Faith, NY, Harper & Row).

Formally speaking, I argue that the logic of deduction and decision is primarily a matter of language (sermocinalis scientia) and presupposes the meaning of signs. John Venn was concerned, as I also worry, about what he calls the "compartmental" import of existential propositions which do not depend on the logical state of member terms that makes them true. Similarly, it is not merely the terms of conscientious assertions that concerns me, because I'm interested in the socio-emotional implication, impact or sensible capacity they might carry. I am fascinated by the modal idiom of assertions concerning which states of affairs "might" happened to occur and modal connectives, such as "A might ø", "A could have ø", "A would or ought ø if", etc. Theophrastus, I think, produced a logic that omitted this sort of contingency. Nonetheless, the feeling among so-called modalists is that possible-world semantics is entirely harmless. Modal propositions assume dispositional predicates of individual things (such as "can break", or "is breakable") as well as dispositional suffixes (such as dissolves, ignites, or solubility, flammability, etc.), explaining 'reasons' and dispositions. Chinese philosophy produced a school of thought (Mo Tzu) which used three tests to unlock the logical validity of statements. For them, truth depended on authority, common observation or practical effect, and I also think that experience and perspective must direct logic.

A dispositional predicate is true simply by virtue of what properties in the world would makes it so. The rub, however, is that 'actuality' changes with time and possibilities also pass. The 'actual' past might be considered linearly, as actualized possibilities, but the future branches into surprising fractals of things that may or may not happen to occur (to-one). There is no shortage of objective physical facts to account for the truth of "might" propositions with regard to personkinds of course (especially across life-time/world). The difficult thing is to be sure which facts are responsible, or which are the facts that are necessary for the relevant possibility to be. For instance, in order to know what facts are responsible for the truth at time T of "A might have ø'ed" one has to know the properties which A possessed at some earlier time (T_e), which, if it goes on to have ø'ed would be the *reason* for A ø'ing.

It is undeniably the case, I think, that the ambitions and disappointments of human lifetimes rest on what might have been (or could be), because personkinds will not settle for less than is barely enough 'good' (if not as much 'right') to make do.

Ludwig Wittgenstein contributed mightily to the study of logic, and his ideas must be respected with regard to the 'truth' of arguments (propositional calculus), of course. He had no "pure" logic nor affection for the logic popularized by Bertrand Russell and Alfred North Whitehead; placing him in the "intuitionist" camp in the opinion of mathematicians. He insisted that all intelligible discourse is restricted to (1) tautologies, or it involves

(2) contradictions or is constructed of (3) descriptive propositions that assert that certain states of affairs do or do not exist; which makes sense to me.

In the service of unassailable "truths", including ideas that are outmoded, unreliable, mistook or simply misleading, we are compelled to decide what we should do about them, if anything. We must determine, for instance, what conduct to dedicate to the cause of cooperative industry and how much to give to social reform, and consider whether that conduct is 'good' (or is suitable within Anglo-American liberal society). I find the sliding around of the meaning of symbols/representations from one set of verbal-ideological circumstances (horizon) to another also makes the terms of daily obligation (reasons to act) slippery.

SUCH TALK...

I'd like to offer an example of my own typical diatribe about current political controversies on public policy and to invite whatever hermeneutic analysis that might be made of it.

"In the multi-cultural neighborhoods in America with which I am familiar, I often encounter proponents of questionable law-enforcement methods supposedly intended to "protect and serve" the public. This can apparently be accomplished by freeing the subverted community from dangerous characters identified as subverting social enclaves (especially the predominantly African-American) under their jurisdiction. This is required in order to keep the peace that law establishes, apparently at the expense of the dignity of threatened citizenry. Thereupon, encouraged by clearly flawed statistical 'evidence' regarding crime rates and their causes, civil officers take up unjust, discriminatory and/or overly disrespectful tactics (such as, "data-driven policing" and "stop and frisk" policies) intended to militate against a contrived criminality insinuated in the community and expecting the surrender of psycho-social and/or economic facts to misplaced force."

Talk like this carries with it a galaxy of energetic socio-emotional points, I think, through which one can reason their way around the life-time/space they find leading in many different directions. Of course, where the tautology of flawed political reasoning I've tried to describe might fail logical muster, the point I hope to make is that convoluted theses can remain persuasive, if illogical, given the appropriate cloud of curious verbal-ideological presuppositions and postulates.

I indorse the idea that public service cannot achieve what is "good" for society without the permission or sanction of those served, and surely not by making the mistake of thoughtless offenses directed toward those who should be better served. The intensity of my feelings about abuse of police authority is born of a common experience among my contemporaries and easily understood by them. There was institutional and official 'apartheid' of law-and-order policies in many American states, and the social problems of the Midwest region in which I lived were as insidious, if not as vicious, as others. Societal 'activists' of my era, who modelled enlightened perception and action, were inspiring for me and the desegregation and anti-poverty initiatives of my era have been passably effective over time.

Socio-emotional disturbances and surges, like my personal aspirations, have roiled, and the grammar of rebellious struggle and stubborn repression remain familiar (horizontally) today, as would be expected, across many verbal-ideological landscapes. Linguistic 'analysis' of my expressions/representations, regardless of time or place must, I think, be primarily concerned with demonstration, elucidation and/or usage rather than definitional reduction to some nonlinguistic 'meaning' (as Wittgenstein discovered). And, for that reason, it is noological discoveries that I find the most intriguing.

Nevertheless, although misery and misunderstanding are never in short supply (either intensifying or numbing so, according to the senses and situations that produce it), it is generally appreciated that respectful sensitivity and societal solicitude make for the most comforting conditions. Moreover, it has been common sense for me to think that the underprivileged and socially insecure laboring classes, where I've been tiresomely occupied, must try to find a modicum of ease in circumstances overcrowded with miseries. This is done as a function of how we eke out accommodations and opportunities and, consequently, are emotionally punished or rewarded ('prosper'). "Eke", in the way I mean to use it comes from an old verb meaning to add, supplement, or grow. I argue that the civil servant's charge is to guard the life-time/spaces within which townspeople try to grow, but not to invade their privacy or abuse authority over them simply to insure socio-economic privilege. As for abuse of authority (even "police brutality") inferred in my rant; it is commonly recognized that such behavior has occurred (loosely defined as any instance in which a police officer or public servant might use excessive or unreasonable force or undue influence). It so happens that during my youth, defiant cultural demonstrations of 'self-defense' and countercultural resistance clashed with law enforcement agents, resulting in a famously 'long, hot summer' of discontent. At that time, I declared that

Martin Luther King, Jr., was astute when he said: "I have tried to offer desperate, rejected, and angry young men my deepest compassion while maintaining my conviction that social change comes most meaningfully through nonviolent action. But, I knew that I could never again raise my voice against the violence of the oppressed in the ghettos without having first spoken clearly to my own government."

Society, as I see it, is in abundant degree positive of personkindness (involving what doing is "right" under given circumstances); whereas it might otherwise have been thought to encompass our aggregate being, instead. I propose that the idea of 'social presence' is important here (moreso than whether many persons make up some nebulous social 'whole').

The social philosopher Burke, for instance, would have us reason clearly about what 'society' means in terms of who it has been decided that a person in it will do, whereas Payne would have one envision who persons might become and how society be. My inclination is to agree with Payne, by the way. My societal worries are still bound up in the dissertations of thinkers like those two and their contemporaries, but I'm sure neither could take a step outside of the verbal-ideological life-timescapes they knew (however much they pushed to expand it, or tucked it up around themselves). The Anglo-American liberal republic of socio-emotional agents with whom I speak are freely committed to both vigorous debate and diligent cooperation, and would harshly criticize any coercion or repression imposed by a privileged few upon a beleaguered many in our polite discourse.

So, if some sense can be got from my musing about how one-self might be and where the likely logical bounds for-oneself (modal personkindness) might be set; I'm afraid that the parataxic quality of intelligence over one's lifetime leaves me puzzled. Nonetheless, by simple employment of familiar language, I find that I can at least somehow convey the conceptual network I call a 'lifetime', regardless of whether I am then faced with the baffling notions, such as 'agent' and 'action', or 'intention' and 'reflection', that mark it.

What may be needed most is for me to explain how dialogic interchanges touch on what I've thought of as 'conscience'. I'd also go so far as to suggest that when sophisticated polemics and rhetoric can be entertained in 'polite society' it might be in relation to how well semantic depth is plumbed there. I must admit, of course, that neither conversational subtlety nor poetic penchant have been reliable meters of keen logic or of 'good' character for that matter, however much delightful.

Adam Smith, an Enlightenment thinker, in his "Theory of Moral Sentiments" reminds me that "How selfish soever man may be supposed, there are evidently some principles in his nature which interest him in the fortune of others and render their happiness necessary to him, though he derives nothing from it except the pleasure of seeing it." I'm not as sure as Smith that a "vile maxim of the masters of mankind" is contested by a more benign "original passion of human nature" that might compensate for some wicked pathology; but I do try to be a moral man.

I must think about my social 'role' (acts) as I try to gage the reach of my individual "personal" state relative to others rightly. Sometimes it may be the case that I hope to arise wealthy or to build wealth and, as the likelihood of that literally diminishes, for many personal reasons my imagination will provide me incentives of that kind. If I can find out what a 'majority' of my contemporaries say they might do, as well, however diffracted my part of their visualization may be, I will struggle to assimilate or rebel against them as a result of the socio-emotional intercourse in which we are engaged. Interestingly enough, Frankl thought that striving for a "clear conscience" in any given situation is a doomed effort and reveals an impossible ambition. He sees such futility as a Pharisaic kind of 'perfectionism' (with which I surely cannot identify). The often quoted German saying: "a good conscience is the best pillow", Frankl reminds me, emphasizes the idea that 'morality' (conscience) does not provide any tranquilizing drug or sleeping pill that will relieve the headache of hard reasoning; and I agree.

I know about the vocabulary of social "identity" that is common now (about who are the poorer or richer, stronger or weak), and has always been culturally shaded and colored by class and race (as I see it). Talking about the political "liberty" we might fashion for-ourselves would be almost incomprehensible, I fear, without an idea of where/when and by whom such conversation is taken up. American-English transforms itself fluently through the capricious bandying about of imprecise and coded utterances, and one cannot easily decode its uses.

I have taken artless stabs at hermeneutic analysis, judged from my personal verbal-ideological perspective, such as the following example: "They claim to be super-patriots, but they would destroy every liberty guaranteed by the Constitution. They demand free enterprise, but are spokesmen for monopoly and vested interest. Their final objective toward which all their deceit is directed is the capture of political power so that, using the power of the state and of the market simultaneously, they may keep the common man in eternal subjection", and I make what meaning out of these assertions I can. The "they" referred to is surely the well-heeled and affluent in the society with which I am familiar enough to comment. Many respected forbearers who I might invoke make similar argument; for instance, Samuel Adams wrote: "It is not infrequent to hear men declaim loudly upon liberty, who, if we may judge by the whole tenor of their actions, mean nothing else by it but their own liberty—to oppress without control or the restraint of laws all who are poorer or weaker than themselves".

Wilhelm von Humboldt, by the way, a founder of so-called 'classical liberalism', wrote about the leading principle towards which every conversation converges being the essential importance of helpful human discourse (in all its richness and diversity). It follows that any effort to restrict the development of discourse is not just intellectually dangerous, or deceitful, but our concern for the common 'good' impels us to find ways to better cultivate the richness of dialogical expression, I feel.

I'm told that 'classical liberalism, as loosely used in American-English is what Rudolf Rocker, a 20th century anarchist thinker, would describe as "a definite trend in the historic dialogue of mankind that strives for the free unhindered development of all the individual and social forces in life". However, there are contemporary intellectuals who have abandoned unfortunately the fight for the ethical 'high ground' of that sort, or venture where any commonality might plant its flag. Almost any serious regard for "common" wants and needs (conviviality) seems to me to have been consigned to near irrelevance in current political debate. And, the once revered temperament of 'willing conciliation' has almost been written out of the serious political dialogue. But, my own stubborn insubordination in this regard, as would be expected of me, remains tenacious. Irremediably cynical types refuse to acknowledge any 'moral sense' or concede to the demands of 'conscientiousness' at all. Political intercourse has become unreliable, at best, or unfruitful at all. Disappointment, dissatisfaction and intolerable disregard have held terrible sway in my recent memory (and sorely tried my patience). Apparently, conscience has become weak and venality prevails, while no fond resolution of societal decline is to be expected. And, I hope we can remedy this glum state of mind.

My contemporaries often find themselves arguing about the proper character or inescapable responsibilities of national compatriots (from the Latin patriōta, meaning "fellow countryman", and from the Ancient Greek πατριώτης or patriotēs also meaning "of the same country" or "compatriot" from the French). The word patriot was previously an ironic term of ridicule and derision in England meaning "a factious disturber of the government". Horace Walpole said "... the most popular declaration which a candidate could make on the hustings was that he had never been and never would be a patriot". A rascally person might also have formerly been called a patrioteer in reference to resistance movements in overrun countries in World War II. But, the idea of patriotism has been revived, nevertheless, and given a positive sense in the American-English with which I am familiar. Whatever the depth of rebellious fervor, it is the fulfillment of a patriotic interest in "liberty" that is meant to be the motivation for it (or so they say).

INDEX

1. Richard Wollheim, The Thread of Life, Harvard U., 1984

2. Eli Hirsch, The Concept of Identity, Oxford U

3. Alvin Plantiga and Saul Kripke, Naming, Necessity and Natural Kinds, Cornell Univ., 1977

4. Baruch Brody, Identity & Essence, Princeton U, 1980

5. Danah Zohar, The Quantum Self, William Morrow & Co., 1990

6. J. Williams Miller, W.W. Norton & Co.,

    (a) Midworld of Symbols and Functioning Objects, 1982

    (b) The Task of Criticism, 2005.

7. Heidegger and Psychology, Review of Existential Psychology & Psychiatry, Eugene Gendin, 1988.

8. George Herbert Mead, (The Social Self, Journal of Phil, Psych & Scientific Methods, 1913.

9. Ideas of Pure Phenomenology, Edmund Husserl, Allen & Unwin, 1958.

10. The Philosophy of Symbolic Forms III, Ernst Cassirer, Yale U, 1985.

11. Phenomenology of Spirit, G.W.F. Hegel, AV Miller, Oxford U. Press, 1977 and Hegel's Philosophy of Right, T.M. Knox translator, Oxford U. Press, 1967

12. The Conscious Universe, Menas Kafatos & Robert Nadeau, Springer-Verlag pub., 1990.

13. They Saw A Game: A Case Study, The Nature of Human Consciousness, Hastorf & Cantril, Viking Press, 1974.

14. The Social Construction of Reality, Peter Berger & Thomas Lackmann, Doubleday, 1967.

15. Simulated Deliberation, Joseph J. Schwab, Univ. Chicago Press, 1969.

16. Experience, Emerson Essays and Lectures, Library of America, 1983.

17. (Christine Korsgaard, The Sources of Normativity).

18. Ivana Markova, Dialogicality and Social Representations: The Dynamics of Mind. Cambridge Univ. Press, 2003

19. Michael Schwalbe, The Sociologically Examined Life, Pieces of the Conversation, No. Carolina State U, Mayfield Publishing, 2001, 1998.

20. Nahmias, Morris, Nadelhoffer and Turner (Phenomenology of Free Will, Journal of Consciousness Studies, 2004)

21. Donald Davidson, Actions and Events, Oxford, 1980

22. James Hopkins, Philosophical Essays on Freud, Cambridge U., 1982

23. Thomas Nagel, Equality and Partiality, Oxford U. Press, 1991

24. T.S. Elliot, The Sacred Wood, Essays on Poetry, Locke Lectures, "Tradition and The Individual Talent", 1922

25. Social Psychology textbook (Brehm, Kassin and Fein, Hougton Mifflin Co., 2005)

26. Viktor Frankl, Man's Search for Meaning, Washington Square Press, 1963

27. From Mikhail Bakhtin, Speech Genres and Other Late Essays. Trans. Vern W. McGee: Univ of Texas Press, 1986

28. Honoria Wells (Phenomenology of Acts of Choice, 1920

30. JH Randall, Jr., The Role of Knowledge in Western Religion

AFTERWARD

I must apologize for the steps in my studies that have been given somewhat short shrift and remain incomplete. Although, it is not clear to me what a shrift is, I know a short one must not be good. I'm told shrift was a word used for a religious confession (something one might want to keep short) or a penance imposed by a priest (something one would definitely wish to keep short) or from the practice of allowing a little time for the condemned to make a confession before being executed. And, I think it would be best, in this case, to make my final summary short.

It is clear to me that concepts and contracts of common consent and civil rule flow from the swell of many familiar psycho-social processes and moral/effective principals. When contemporary science and common practice have shown the interconnectedness of conditions and circumstances our risk aversion to reliance and conditioned mistrusts work against our best interests. Where the dialogic tributaries that feed life (some bitter or acid, others viscous and rich) are dammed and/or cut off, the people perish. The racial codification, gaping

Rudolph McNair

class disparities and/or political subjugation of persons produces a treacherous institutional/business ethic which does us no good.

I think that the world comes to us, and we live in it composing a conversation/song of consciousness; and our capacities and passions are nourished by others' love. If we participate in the 'divine' undertaking (God's love) then our want to be sustained, or have our presence valued by other personkinds (and to likewise nourish them) then I've suggested that autonomy of self (in-itself) is not central to our being (personkindness) but, otherwise, tangential to it.

I've concluded that personkinds require a psyhco-social and dialogic component with that is fluid across language groups. The important point to make, I think, is that the life-time/world we know is unremittingly challenging for us to describe and explain, but we must accept that challenge. I know that my life-time/world demands at least ample daring to brave a foggy future and enough stubborn insolence to complicate the certainty of the recent past. Just as Sartre provided us no existential exit from insecurity, I admit no reliance on fate nor will I surrender to simple positivism here.

I further propose that experiences (senses) of things are in curious flux throughout the knowing cosmos, where I assume there is no unfulfilled "space". Although time and place shift relative to the clarity of one's point of view, one can, nonetheless, fulfill the potential and meaning of events through unrelenting verbal-ideological interchange (or forfeit invitation to 'events' altogether).

I've supposed that the first burble of one-mind's self is but a wonted proof of "feeling" (just strong enough to tell about) eager for an echo from somewhere another splashes. I've imagined life-world horizons that radiate with apperception of every element of "truth" (complimentary to some other such element), and everywhere those elements will have cogent 'syntony' but not necessarily require linear or chronological succession.

I've entrusted personkindness with the awakening of vital willpower, for good reason. And, I've concluded that neither quavering biotic sentience boiling with fluent oxytosins nor waves of nervous passion pulsing through life-world are satisfactory facts for explaining one-self's mind or help decide when personkindness rightly takes its place, for me. The cloudy dialogical process engulfs and whelms my lifetime, commonly dousing places where we touch with the cool, slippery hints of meaning.

I still wonder whether we can ever successfully retrieve some former "meaning" of utterances, especially when they involve such notions as "patriot", or "liberty", echoing from lost verbal-ideological times and spaces, or if we can step into the same perceptual rivers in which those "meanings" once flowed. Can we be certain, for instance, what the proper "punishments" of capital crimes are or mean to achieve? Many assumptions about meaning are likely to dwell within the spiritual core of political ravings such as those most familiar to me. I suspect there are whole texts of "meaningful" verses that inhabit many dialogical moments, epochs or spans of lifetime familiar to me. It remains debatable, nonetheless, whether all symbols/signs are fundamentally inter-dimensional (always operating freely between socio-ideological universes) or some are world-bound or time-distinct.

If the reader will excuse the intellectual mischief I've made so far, I hope to have kept honestly to the seeker's path. Although I am never without doubt or suspicion, however much my brain may contrive conceptual deceits or I might fall into illusion, but I'm convinced that it is discourse (especially of this philosophical sort) itself that provides "mind" sure footing and sets for us each a secure place to be.

I pray that the words of my mouth and the meditations of my spirit will be acceptably loving, and that whatsoever things are true and of good report, in God's sight, I will wish to do. I'm sure that there is no willpower that can gather the whole of my private 'self' without the reflection of personkindliness grasped in association with others. And so, I perpetually construct the 'good' (for reasons not entirely my own) that I should do in conversation/ intercourse with others.

Carol Ochs (The Song of the Self, Trinity Press, 1994) instructs us thusly: "We associate self-consciousness with discomfort and unease. We tend to notice something – the foot, the heart – when it is not working right, but when it is well, it escapes our attention. Sot it is with the self, but the self usually is not working right, thereby obstructing our free, unself-conscious use of it. We should aim then to cease focusing on the self in order to be free simply to use it. The self is not unreal, it should just not be the object of our consciousness. If we learn to get the self 'out of the way', we can become one with what we wish to learn." However, I'm sure she does not mean we should ignore the 'self' altogether. For instance, she goes on to explain that the "no self" encountered in eastern philosophies is not meant to divide the self from the consciousness of the self or a denial of the identity of the self. "A pianist who no longer pays conscious attention to the separate motions of the fingers is not someone who no longer has fingers, but someone whose fingers function so well that the consciousness can focus entirely on the music. When we finally 'get out of the way', our consciousness can focus on the music around us." Much like Danah Zohar proposed with regard to quantum consciousness, Ochs informs us; "We not only have a self, in the process of living we become aware of a multiplicity of selves. At times of creativity or intuition, something seems to be living through us, or, as Freud wrote, 'I am lived'." Finally, she determines that, having accepted and integrated the many aspects of the self we can undertake the disintegration of the boundaries of the self: "If I am only for myself, what am I?" she asks.

I, myself quest for the place where I can locate myself within the processes/experiences that my personkindness settles upon. I commend the integration of person kinds and compassion for other selves good reason (as I am not existentially nor morally 'whole' without these necessary conditions). Self-protection and risk aversion have become a key frame in political discourse, of late, implying a sense of individual control over exposure to dangerous circumstances, I'm afraid, and the focus is shifted away from collective forms of protection from universal risks. However, I insist that individualization of risk is inept, if not hurtful, especially in light of divergent personal perspective and disparate communicative arrangements (historical and demographic).